Natural Remedies:

An Everyday Guide to Herbal Teas, Infusions & Decoctions

A handy and quick A-Z home reference for understanding and using the healing power of nature

The Authors

Durga Nath Dhar, Ph.D., F.N.A.Sc., is an expert in natural products and synthetic organic chemistry. He retired from the Department of Chemistry, Indian Institute of Technology, Kanpur, after 35 years of distinguished academic life. He has over 130 research papers, articles and books to his credit. He is a member of several professional and learned societies and has served on the scientific advisory committee of the Central Council for Research in Unani Medicine, Ministry of Health and Family Welfare, Government of India. Professor Dhar is a recipient of the fellowship of the National Academy of Sciences. In recognition of his contributions to science, his name is included in *The International Directory of Distinguished Leadership, 1990.*

Rupa Dhar, M.A., B.Sc., B.Ed., was principal and science co-ordinator of the campus school at the Indian Institute of Technology, Kanpur, where she specialised in elementary science education. She has been an active member of the All India Science Teachers' Association, and her interests include child education, child psychology and folklore medicine.

The authors would welcome suggestions and comments about the book from readers; including their personal experiences with herbal teas. These maybe sent to Natural Remedies: An Everyday Guide to Herbal Teas, Infusions & Decoctions c/o Orient Paperbacks, Madarsa Road, Kashmere Gate, Delhi-110 006.

Natural Remedies

An Everyday Guide to Herbal Teas, Infusions, and Decoctions

DN Dhar • Rupa Dhar

Disclaimer

This book has been designed to provide information and to educate. The authors and Orient Paperbacks shall have neither liability nor responsibility to any person or entity with respect to any loss, damage, or injury caused or alleged to be caused directly or indirectly by the information in this book. The information presented herein is in no way intended to substitute or replace medical counselling.

How to Order

This book is available on special quantity discounts from the publisher Orient Paperbacks, Madarsa Road, Kashmere Gate, Delhi-110 006. Tel. +91-(011) 386 2267, 386 2201, Fax.:+91-11-386 2935 email: mail@orientpaperbacks.com. In your message kindly include information concerning the intended use of the book and the number of copies you wish to purchase.

www.orientpaperbacks.com
email: mail@orientpaperbacks.com

ISBN 81-222-0319-1
1st Published in Orient Paperbacks 2002

Natural Remedies: An Everyday Guide to Herbal Teas, Infusions & Decoctions

Cover design by Vision Studio

Published by
Orient Paperbacks
(A division of Vision Books Pvt. Ltd.)
Madarsa Road, Kashmere Gate, Delhi-110 006

Printed in India at
V. K. Printers, New Delhi-110 020

Cover Printed at
Ravindra Printing Press, Delhi-110 006

Preface

Scientific literature is replete with examples of how the medicinal properties of herbs and plants have been effectively used not only to heal and rejuvenate the sick, but also to protect the healthy against diseases and infections. These healing qualities of herbs have been scientifically confirmed. The illustrative examples are: foxglove and rauwolfia for the management of blood pressure; *Vinca rosea*, *Taxus baccata* in the treatment of cancer; ephedra in the treatment of asthma; senna for constipation; *chirayata* for restoring appetite; turmeric for inflammatory conditions ... the list is almost endless.

Experience has shown that crude extracts of some medicinal herbs have a superior curative action than preparations containing the purified bio-active compound. One of the authors, during his tenure as a visiting scientist at the Shemyakin Institute of Bio-organic Chemistry, USSR Academy of Sciences, Moscow, in 1977, was requested by a colleague, a steroid chemist and a hypertensive patient, to arrange from India tablets prepared from the crude extract of the herb *Rauwolfia serpentina*. She explained that she preferred the crude extract over the readily available pure drug, Reserpine, which though effective in bringing down her blood pressure, was always associated with a 'hangover', an unpleasant side effect. This she attributed to the pure drug. On an earlier visit to India, she had taken the crude drug as a pill, and had experienced a feeling of well being, with no side effects! Her conclusion was scientific yet simple: the crude drug contains, besides Reserpine, several other related substances which obviate the unpleasant side effects of Reserpine.

There are many advantages of using medicinal herbs. They are inexpensive, therapeutically effective, and without any unpleasant side effects. Even if they do not relieve the condition fully, they do no harm.

These time-tested herbal medicines, also often referred to as 'household' remedies, are useful for the treatment of day-to-day illnesses — minor coughs, common cold, indigestion, sore throat and intestinal worms.

For best results herbal remedies should be initiated in the early stages of the disease. The treatment may be continued if there are signs of improvement; otherwise professional medical advice should be sought. It must be remembered that herbal medicine should be considered an adjunct to, and not a substitute of, modern medicine. For a disease requiring emergency treatment and quick effect, powerful modern medicine would be the correct choice.

In writing this book, the authors have drawn freely on information from various sources and wish to acknowledge their indebtedness to the authors and publishers of these books. Thanks are also due to the director, Central Institute of Medicinal and Aromatic Plants (CIMAP), Lucknow, for allowing us access to the library, to Dr Akhtar Hussain, ex-director, CIMAP, for his valuable suggestions, and to Prof. G.N. Pandey, for his continued interest and help during the writing of this book.

Last, but not least, the authors thank Nikhil, Surinder, Preeti, Pankaj, Paarth and Sonali for their patience.

Durga Nath Dhar
Rupa Dhar

Contents

The Herbal Heritage

The use of herbs as medicine dates back to antiquity. Intimate knowledge of the medicinal properties of herbs came to the ancients by direct observation, insight, experience, and by trial and error. The *Atharva veda* contains descriptions about the use of herbs for health and healing as was practised by the ancient Aryans. This scientifically documented body of knowledge, known as the Ayurvedic system of medicine, relies heavily on the healing properties of herbs and plants. Other systems of alternate medicine which are primarily based on herbal remedies are the Graeco-Arab (*Unani*), Homeopathy and *Siddha*.

India possesses vast resources of medicinal plants which constitute the principal source of drugs used in the indigenous systems of medicine. It is estimated that more than 8000 medicinal plants are used in India and South East Asia, while China uses around 5,000 plant remedies. In the UK, about 2,600 products obtained from some 280 herbs are sold as herbal remedies. In many other European countries, herbal medicines are equally popular.

Traditional systems of medicine offer time-tested remedies. All remedies can be made at home with ease, using spices, vegetables, fruits and flowers found in the kitchen, in the backyard or the garden. Some herbal remedies are used to enhance longevity, delay ageing, improve immunity, develop body resistance, improve mental faculties and add vitality and lustre to the body. Traditional remedies have also been used for a wide range of effects, such as analgesics, sedatives, anthelmintics, antirheumatics and antiasthmatics.

For a large part of the world's population, traditional herbal medicine has been, and still is, the only form of medicare available. In India, where a sizeable percentage of the population is poor, herbal medication is an inexpensive and effective alternative. Practitioners of herbal medicine, commonly known as *Vaidyas* and *Hakims*, constitute an important part of the country's health care system and enjoy a high degree of acceptance and respect.

Safe and Soothing

The rapid advances made by modern medicine have, in some ways, overshadowed traditional and home remedies. As a result, many people have come to believe that herbal medicine is mere folklore and are sceptical about its efficacy.

Modern medicine has limited applications and does not offer a satisfactory solution for many chronic ailments: even if such solutions are available, they provide only temporary relief with attendant side effects. The undesirable side effects and the toxic nature of modern drugs are major health concerns. The indigenous systems of medicine, on the other hand, use cures that are safe and free from side effects, and many of these are based on sound scientific principles.

Many herbs used in traditional medicine have now been absorbed, assimilated and adopted by modern medicine. In this context, it is important to remember that herbs constitute the single biggest source of pharmaceutically useful drugs. A recent survey in the USA revealed that about 50 per cent of the modern medicines used today by clinicians are of plant origin. Any prejudice against home remedies would therefore be unfair and unwarranted. Perhaps the most effective approach towards health care would be to combine the simple but effective traditional practices with sophisticated modern therapeutics.

Preparing Herbal Teas

The extract of medicinal plants or herbs in water is called 'tea', or more precisely, *tisane*. Preparing *tisane* is the simplest way of extracting therapeutically active substances from medicinal plants.

Medicinal herbs, as the name implies, contain therapeutically useful constituents. To effectively extract the medicinal substance with, and in water, it is necessary either to break the plant material of bark, root and wood into small pieces, or reduce it to powder (leaves, for example). This allows the water to penetrate into the deep-seated vegetable cells and dissolve the therapeutically active constituents therein.

This book contains procedures for preparing herbal teas from over 200 medicinal plants. Each plant is listed by its common name, followed by its botanical or Latin name. Wherever available, the common Indian equivalent is also provided. There is a brief introduction for each disease, including its causes and principal symptoms. This is followed by the method of preparation of herbal teas, either with a single herb, and/or by combining several herbs.

Procuring and Storage of Herbs

Most medicinal herbs are readily available from herbalists or *pansaris*. Alternatively, these medicinal plants may be grown in one's own herbal garden, or obtained from the wild. Care should however be exercised in not collecting plants that have been exposed to pollutants such as automobile exhaust gases, weed killer sprays, or other toxic liquids.

Medicinal plants should be plucked before they come to full flower. This ensures the best aroma and flavour. The ideal time for picking herbs is early morning, as the heat of the sun causes some essential oils to escape into the atmosphere.

As far as possible tea should be made from fresh herbs. If herbs have to be used at a later date, these should be dried at about 35°C before storing. Drying prevents spoilage due to fungal bacterial growth. The dried herbs should be broken into small pieces and stored in airtight glass or foodgrade pet container in a cool, dark place. The stored leaves, flowers and fruits should be used within one year, while the roots, rhizomes and seeds should be used within three years.

Method of Preparation

There are two methods for preparing herbal teas: infusion and decoction. The choice of the method depends upon the part of the plant to be used for extraction — seeds, stem, wood, root, rhizome, flowers, leaves, twigs, etc.

Infusions or decoctions should always be made fresh before use and should not be kept for a prolonged period to prevent the deterioration of the active substances present in the extract.

Infusion

Extraction by infusion is most suitable when less dense parts of the herb are used, i.e. flowers, leaves, twigs, fruits, etc. An infusion is prepared by steeping the herb in hot water. About half a litre or 2 cups of boiling water is poured over 1 to 2 teaspoons of the crushed or ground herb, covered and left for 10 to 15 minutes before straining through a clean muslin cloth or wire mesh strainer. The extract or tea, after the addition of sugar, honey, lemon juice or spices, is ready for administration to the patient.

Decoction

Decoctions are recommended for extracting the water soluble substances from the tougher parts of plants, such as the seed, bark, wood, rhizomes, roots, etc. A decoction is prepared by slowly boiling about 1 teaspoon of powdered herb in a litre of water (4 cups) for half an hour in a covered vessel. The liquid is slowly allowed to cool before straining. According to some prescriptions, the decoction is concentrated to a small volume before being given to the patient.

The residue left after straining the first decoction can be utilised, say, after 10 to 12 hours to make a second decoction by boiling it with an additional quantity of water, followed by its subsequent concentration to a smaller volume, approximately 1/7 of the original.

Selecting the Right Vessel

Stainless steel or glass vessels are best. Aluminium vessels should not be used. Aluminium reacts with organic acids present in some plants and contaminates the tea. Tea should be strained through a clean muslin cloth or a wire strainer.

Preparation Time

The time required for making herbal teas is given in all cases. Where a time range is given, say, 5 to 20 minutes, it indicates the minimum and the maximum allowable time.

Temperature

Temperature plays an important role in the successful extraction of medicinal constituents. For this reason herbs are heated in water for a limited time. In some cases, the biologically active components may be destroyed by prolonged heating. Bearberry is an example in which boiling the plant in water is contraindicated. Boilingnot only destroys the efficacy of the drug but also produces a bitter taste due to the extraction of a large quantity of tannin. Bearberry tea is therefore prepared by soaking its leaves in water. Mucilaginous herbs like linseed and quince, on the other hand, are allowed to remain steeped in boiling water for some time, and then the aqueous macerate is swallowed.

Measurements

Units of measurement expressed in teaspoon, tablespoon, handful or cupful have been used in the book. Although such measurements are less precise than those adopted in modern medicine, they do not materially alter the efficacy of herbal medicine. The healing components of herbs are less concentrated than those found in allopathic medicinal pills or tablets. This allows for a certain latitude in their concentration. There is thus little to worry about the precise measures usually employed in allopathic drugs. Normally, tea prepared with fresh herbs requires three times the quantity of the herb as compared to tea prepared with dried herbs. The quantity of water used should be sufficient to cover the plant material in the vessel. However, where a herb might be harmful if taken in the excess, exact amount has been specified.

Abbreviations used in the book.

tsp	=	teaspoon/teaspoons
tbsp	=	tablespoon/tablespoons
g	=	gram/grams
cm	=	centimetre

Publisher's Note

In the main text of the book each herb is listed first by its common English name, followed by its botanical or Latin name in italics and finally, wherever available by its common Indian name. The remedies are given in alphabetical order.

The term 'natural remedies' refers exclusively to herbal teas. Herbal teas or tisane are really the safest, easiest and the best way to benefit from medicinal properties of plants.

How to Use Herbal Teas

Bitter-tasting herbal teas can be made palatable by adding sugar or honey to them. Teas that produce side effects such as nausea or gripes (senna, for example, which is used for the treatment of constipation), are usually given in combination with aromatics such as cardamoms, cinnamon, and cloves.

The instructions regarding the methods of taking of herbal teas, should be followed. As a rule, raw, cold, greasy and hard-to-digest foods should be avoided while taking herbal teas.

Dosage

Herbal teas have to be used judiciously and the recommended dosage instructions followed. Large dosages of some teas can produce unwanted side effects such as nausea, vomiting and skin eruptions, and should be avoided The elderly, or those suffering from cardiovascular problems, disorders of the stomach, liver and kidney should refrain from continuous and uninterrupted use of liquorice. Parsley tea should not be taken by pregnant women as it may induce an abortion.

It is important to note that all the dosages described in this book are for adults. The dosage for children, in the age group of 1 to 14 years varies approximately from ⅛ to ¾ of the adult dose. Those over 65 years of age should begin with a weaker preparation, increasing the strength of the extract gradually if needed.

Duration of Treatment

The duration of the treatment is generally 2 to 3 weeks. The teas should be taken at the onset and during the course of the disease. The duration of the treatment varies from person to person. If a patient responds positively, it should be continued, otherwise it may be stopped.

Of the several teas and extracts provided for each ailment, the reader is free to select the one for which the ingredients are more readily available in his geographic location.

Herbal Teas, Infusions, and Decoctions

Loss of appetite, or anorexia as it is known medically, is a symptom of several diseases which include gastroenteritis, indigestion, common cold and other infections, as well as alcoholism, tuberculosis, drug abuse and nervous and emotional disorders. If left untreated, anorexia can lead to malnutrition, especially in the elderly.

Loss of appetite in children is a side effect of all fevers and many other disorders.

The condition is characterised by a lack of appetite and an astringent taste in the mouth, associated with bad breath.

CARDAMOM

Elettaria cardamomum Maton
Choti elaichi

Ingredients

Cardamom, powdered	1 g
Water	½ cup

Method

Put the powdered cardamom in ½ cup water and bring the mixture to a boil. Boil for one minute, remove from the heat, let it stand for 10 minutes and then strain.

Preparation time: boiling time 1 minute; standing time 10 minutes.

Dosage

1 tbsp, every 15 minutes till the symptoms disappear.

CHAMOMILE

Anthemis nobilis Linn.
Babunah

Ingredients

Flowers, crushed	1 tsp
Boiling water	1 cup

Method
Combine the boiling water and the flowers in a covered container and allow the tea to stand for 5-10 minutes. Discard the flowers by straining the extract through a muslin cloth or any other suitable strainer, and drink the freshly prepared watery extract 3-4 times a day. *Preparation time: 5–10 minutes.*

Dosage
1 cup, 3-4 times a day.

HOLY BASIL

Ocimum sanctum
Tulsi

Ingredients

Leaves, crushed	11 g
Water	2 cups
Milk	1 tbsp
Sugar	15 g

Method
Boil the leaves in 2 cups water in a covered container and cook till the water is reduced to 1 cup. Strain and add milk and sugar and garnish with powdered cardamoms.
Preparation time: 15 minutes.

Dosage
1 cup, 3 times a day.

JUNIPER

Juniperus communis Linn.
Abbhal /Aaraar

Ingredients

Berries, branches, wood, finely chopped	1 tsp
Boiling water	1 cup

Method

Combine the chopped herb and the boiling water in a container, cover and let the tea brew for 20 minutes. Strain and drink morning and evening. *Preparation time: 20 minutes.*

Dosage

1 cup, twice a day.

Caution: This tea is not recommended for pregnant and nursing women.

PEPPERMINT

Mentha piperita
Paparaminta

Ingredients

Recently dried leaves, crushed	15 g
Boiling water	2 cups

Method

Infuse the herb in boiling water for 5-20 minutes, depending on the concentration required. Strain the infusion before drinking. *Preparation time: 5-20 minutes.*

Dosage

1-2 cups a day between meals, hot or warm.

Caution: This tea should not be given to infants or very young children as they may experience an unpleasant choking sensation.

Appetite, Loss of (Anorexia)

ROSEMARY

Rosmarinus officinalis Linn
Rusmary

Ingredients

Leaves, crushed	1 tsp
Boiling water	1 cup

Method

To prepare the tea, place the leaves in a container and pour the boiling water over them. Cover the container and let the leaves steep in the water for 10 minutes. Strain, and the tea is ready. *Preparation time: 10 minutes.*

Dosage

1 cup, twice a day.

FENNEL + MINT + ROSE

Foeniculum vulgare + *Mentha aruensis* + *Rosa damascene*
Saunf + Pudina + Gulab

Ingredients

Fennel seeds, crushed	6 g
Mint leaves, crushed	6 g
Rose flower, crushed	6 g
Boiling water	¾ cup

Method

Combine the three herbs and pour the boiling water over them. Let the mixture stand in a covered vessel for 30 minutes, then strain the tea and drink twice a day.
Preparation time: 30 minutes.

Dosage

¾ cup, twice a day.

Arteriosclerosis, or the hardening of the arteries, is usually a disease of middle and old age.

Fatty deposits develop on the walls of the blood vessels in the arteries causing them to harden. Later, these deposits may enlarge and form plaques, leading to the narrowing of the arteries. This arterial narrowing, known as arteriosclerosis, interferes with the free circulation of blood. The clotting of blood wherever plaques occur is known as arterial thrombosis.

The manifestation of arteriosclerosis is usually seen in older patients, but young people too are susceptible to it. Arteriosclerosis could be a result of persistent high blood pressure, diabetes, acute infectious diseases, gout, rheumatism and kidney disease. Heredity also plays an important role in arteriosclerosis. It is known to run in families where the young are its victims.

Arteriosclerosis leads to a defective blood supply to vital organs like the brain and the heart. In the brain, it may cause the impairment of mental functions and lead to a stroke, which is the paralysis of a part or all of one side of the body (apoplexy), and unconsciousness. The narrowing of the coronary arteries of the heart causes a decrease in the supply of blood and oxygen, which predisposes the patient to excruciating chest pain, known as *Angina pectoris,* and heart attack.

When the flow of blood in the legs is affected, patients may experience excruciating pain while walking.

Serveral herbal teas are effective in relieving the problems associated with arteriosclerosis.

ARTICHOKE

Cynara scolymus
Hatichak

Ingredients

Dry leaves, crushed	1–2 tsp
Water	1 cup

Method

Boil the artichoke leaves in the water for 1 minute, remove from the heat, cover and let stand for 5-10 minutes. Strain before drinking. *Preparation time: boiling time 1 minute; standing time 5–10 minutes.*

Dosage

1 cup, 2-3 times a day for one week.

EUROPEAN MISTLETOE

Viscum album
Banda

Ingredients

Dried branches, shredded	2–3 tsp
Water	1 cup

Method

Put the shredded branches of the European mistletoe into the water, cover and allow the mixture to stand for 8 hours. Strain the tea and drink morning and evening.
Preparation time: 8 hours.

Dosage

1 cup, twice a day for several weeks.

GINKGO

Ginkgo biloba

Ingredients

Leaves, crushed	2–3 tsp
Boiling water	1 cup

Method

Mix the boiling water and leaves in a container, cover and let the mixture stand for 15 minutes. Strain the tea and discard the leaves. *Preparation time: 15 minutes.*

Dosage

1 cup, twice a day.

HAWTHORN

Crataegus oxycantha

Ban sangli

Ingredients

Dried blossoms, crushed	1 tsp
Dried leaves, crushed	1 tsp
Boiling water	1 cup

Method

To prepare the tea, combine all three ingredients including the boiling water in a suitable container, cover and allow the tea to brew for 20 minutes. Strain the extract and sweeten with a little honey or sugar if desired. *Preparation time: 20 minutes.*

Dosage

1 cup, 2-3 times a day for several weeks/months.

Helpful hint: Hawthorn tea shows positive results when used over a prolonged period.

Arteriosclerosis

ROSEMARY

Rosmarinus officinalis

Rusmary

Ingredients

Leaves, crushed	1 tsp
Boiling water	1 cup

Method

In a covered pan, steep the rosemary leaves in the boiling water for 10 minutes. Then strain the infusion and drink twice a day, only in the daytime. *Preparation time: 10 minutes.*

Dosage

1 cup, twice a day for several weeks during the daylight hours only.

LAVENDER + ROSEMARY

Lavandula angustifolia + Rosmarinus officinalis

Dharu + Rusmary

Ingredients

Lavender, whole plant, crushed	½ tsp
Rosemary, whole plant, crushed	½ tsp
Boiling water	1 cup

Method

Combine the two herbs and pour the boiling water over them, cover the container and let the mixture stand for 10–15 minutes. Strain the tea and drink as directed.
Preparation time: 10–15 minutes.

Dosage

1 cup, morning and evening for several weeks.

Asthma is a chronic disorder of the respiratory system and is characterised by difficulty in breathing, wheezing, and a feeling of tightness in the chest. It is caused by the narrowing of the small bronchial passages, or air tubes leading to the lungs, as a result of inflammation or the accumulation of phlegm.

Some of the causes of asthma are respiratory infections, allergy to dust or pollens, viral infections, allergy to chemicals, colds and emotional stress.

An asthma attack lasts for several hours and may be followed by prolonged coughing, wheezing and breathlessness. The following herbal teas may provide some relief.

EPHEDRA

Ephedra vulgaris

Asmania

Ingredients

Whole plant, bruised	14 g
Boiling water	2 cups

Method

Cover the bruised herb with the boiling water and allow the mixture to steep for 15 minutes in a covered container. Strain the tea and drink at room temperature.

Preparation time: 15 minutes.

Dosage

1-2 cups a day.

Caution: Large doses of ephedra may cause a tingling sensation, vomiting, flushing, palpitations, dizziness, insomnia and headaches. People suffering from diabetes, heart conditions and thyroid diseases should avoid excessive use of this herb.

༺ EUCALYPTUS ༻

Eucalyptus globulus
Kapoora maram

Ingredients

Leaves, ground	2 g
Boiling water	2 cups

Method

Put the ground eucalyptus leaves in a suitable container and pour the boiling water over them. Cover the container and let the mixture stand for 5-20 minutes, depending on the strength of the tea desired. Strain and drink at room temperature.
Preparation time: 5-20 minutes.

Dosage

1 cup, twice a day.

༺ GINGER ༻

Zingiber officnale Rosc.
Adrak

Ingredients

Dried powder	¼ tsp
Boiling water	½ cup

Method

Steep the ginger powder in ½ cup boiling water in a covered container for 15 minutes. Strain and drink it warm.
Preparation time: 15 minutes.

Dosage

2 tbsp at bedtime.

HOREHOUND

Marrubium vulgaris
Pahari gandana

Ingredients

Tender shoots, ground	1 tsp
Boiling water	1 cup

Method
Cover the herb with boiling water, close the lid of the pan and leave for 15 minutes, then strain. *Preparation time: 15 minutes.*

Dosage
1 cup a day, 1 tbsp at a time.

NEEM

Azadirachta indica
Neem

Ingredients

Leaves/flowering tops	1 tsp
Boiling water	1 cup

Method
Steep the herb in boiling water in a covered pan for 15 minutes, then strain. *Preparation time: 15 minutes.*

Dosage
1 cup a day, 1 tbsp at a time.

SUNDEW

Drosera rotundifolia
Muka jali

Ingredients

Dried herb, ground	½-1 tsp
Boiling water	1 cup

Method

Mix the ground herb with the boiling water in a container, allow the mixture to stand covered for 5-10 minutes and then strain. When the tea cools to room temperature, it is ready to drink. *Preparation time: 5-10 minutes.*

Dosage

1 cup, twice a day with honey if desired.

Side effects: Sundew imparts a dark colour to the urine – a harmless side effect.

THYME

Thymus vulgaris Linn.
Ajwain

Ingredients

Leaves, ground	1 tsp
Water	1 cup

Method

Warm the mixture of herb and water in a pan, strain and sweeten with honey if desired. *Preparation time: 1 minute.*

Dosage

1 cup, 3 times a day.

Helpful hint: The honey acts as a demulcent, that is, it allays irritation thereby increasing the effectiveness of the tea.

Blood Pressure, High (Hypertension)

Blood pressure values for a normal and healthy individual should be about 120 mm mercury – systolic – and 80 mm mercury – diastolic. The pressure in the arteries when the heart contracts and releases blood into the aorta (main artery) is known as systolic pressure of the blood, whereas the presssure in the arteries when the heart relaxes and expands, filling with blood, is called diastolic pressure.

The two numbers involved in a blood pressure reading are usually written like a fraction: systolic pressure is above or to the left and the diastolic pressure is below or to the right: 120/80. If for some reason, the blood pressure levels are consistently above the normal range, the individual is considered to be hypertensive or suffering from high blood pressure.

Children of hypertensive parents are likely to inherit this disorder. Also, the elderly are generally more prone to hypertension because, with the advancement of age the arteries harden and become narrow when fat and calcium are deposited in them. When this happens the heart has to expend more effort, which leads to high blood pressure.

The symptoms of hypertension include frequent headaches, giddiness, disturbed sleep or insomnia, palpitation, or a faster than normal pulse rate called *Tachycardia*, impaired vision, mental deterioration, confusion, loss of concentration, depression, irritability, weakness, disorders of the digestive system and a gradual loss of body weight.

If the pressure of blood to the brain increases beyond tolerable levels, it may cause a vein to rupture resulting in a cerebral haemorrhage or stroke.

Excessive smoking, anxiety and worry, emotional stress and overwork are other factors that precipitate this condition.

Blood Pressure, High (Hypertension)

ALFALFA

Medicago sativa
Alfalfa

Ingredients

Seeds, crushed	1 tsp
Water	4 cups

Method
Boil the seeds in 4 cups water for 30 minutes and strain. *Preparation time: 30 minutes.*

Dosage
1 cup, 6–7 times a day.

HAWTHORN

Crataegus oxycantha
Ban sangli

Ingredients

Dried blossoms, crushed	1 tsp
Dried leaves, crushed	1 tsp
Boiling water	1 cup

Method
To prepare the tea, combine all three ingredients, including the boiling water, in a suitable container, cover and allow the tea to brew for 20 minutes. Strain the extract and take 2–3 times a day. *Preparation time: 20 minutes.*

Dosage
⅓ cup, 2–3 times a day.

MARIGOLD

Calendula officinalis
Zergul

Ingredients

Flower heads, crushed	1-2 tsp
Boiling water	2 cups

Method
Add the marigold flowers to the boiling water and let them steep, covered, for 15-20 minutes. At the end of the standing time discard the flowers and the tea is ready to drink. *Preparation time: 15–20 minutes.*

Dosage
1 cup, twice a day.

PARSLEY

Petroselinum crispum
Prajmoda

Ingredients

Parsley, chopped	1 tsp
Water	1 cup

Method
Put the chopped parsley in 1 cup water, bring to a boil, then remove from the heat. Let the tea stand for 15 minutes, then strain. *Preparation time: 15 minutes.*

Dosage
1 tbsp, several times a day.

RED PERIWINKLE

Catharanthus roseus Linn.
Sadabahar

Ingredients

Fresh/sun dried leaves, crushed	1 tsp
Water	1 cup

Method

Suspend the leaves in the water and bring to a boil, cover and simmer for 10 minutes, remove from the heat and strain. *Preparation time: 10 minutes.*

Dosage

1 tbsp a day.

Helpful hint: The leaves of the red periwinkle are best when picked before the plant flowers.

STINGING NETTLE

Urtica dioica
Bichhu

Ingredients

Young leaves, chopped	1 handful
Boiling water	2 cups

Method

Mix the leaves in the water, cover the pan and cool the mixture for 15 minutes, then strain. With the addition of a little lemon juice, the tea is ready to drink. *Preparation time: 15 minutes.*

Dosage

¼ cup a day.

Blood Pressure, Low (Hypotension)

When the pressure of the blood within the arteries falls below the normal range (120/80), the condition is known as low blood pressure or hypotension.

Hypotension can be caused by an internal injury such as the rupturing of a stomach ulcer, and external injury such as a severe nosebleed or an accident leading to the loss of blood. Shock, anaemia, leukaemia and chronic diseases can also cause hypotension.

The cardinal symptoms of hypotension are weakness, nausea, cold sweat, giddiness, palpitation and headache.

ROSEMARY

Rosmarinus officinalis Linn.

Rusmary

Ingredients

Fresh/dried leaves, crushed	1 tsp
Boiling water	1 cup

Method

Put the rosemary leaves in a suitable container and pour the boiling water over them. Cover and allow the tea to brew for 5-10 minutes. Strain and serve. *Preparation time: 5-10 minutes.*

Dosage

1 cup, twice a day.

Bronchitis (Acute and Chronic)

Bronchitis is the inflammation of the larger bronchial tubes that carry air to the lungs. Bronchitis may be acute or chronic. The symptoms of acute bronchitis are a persistent cough with occasional wheezing, and shortness of breath. The phlegm may contain pus, making it grey or yellow in colour. Patients may also experience loss of appetite, headache and fever. An attack may last from 1 to 3 weeks.

Chronic bronchitis is a progressive condition in which the air sacs in the lungs are destroyed. These changes restrict the flow of blood through the lungs thus putting strain on the circulation, which may lead to heart failure. The symptoms of chronic bronchitis include a chronic cough with white, frothy spit, increased breathlessness and wheezing, a general feeling of ill health and chest pain.

Bronchitis may result from an allergy to dust, pollen, air-borne mould, as in acute bronchitis, or from an irritation of the bronchial tubes caused by smoke and other injurious chemicals, as in chronic bronchitis. Anyone is susceptible to bronchitis, but children and the elderly are more prone to this disorder.

Herbal teas help in the healing of bronchitis by liquefying the thick mucus and expelling it from the bronchial tubes by inducing coughing.

ELECAMPANE

Inula helenium
Rasan

Ingredients

Root, finely chopped	1–2 tsp
Water	2½ cups

Method
Prepare the decoction by boiling the chopped root for 15-20 minutes. After boiling, let the mixture stand for 15 minutes, strain and drink. *Preparation time: boiling time 15–20 minutes; standing time 15 minutes.*

Dosage
1 cup, twice a day.

HOREHOUND

Marrubium vulgare Linn.
Pahari gandana

Ingredients

Dried flowering plant, ground	1 handful
Water	2 cups

Method
Raise the herb and water mixture to a boil and remove from the heat. Let it stand for 20 minutes, strain and drink when it has cooled. *Preparation time: 20 minutes.*

Dosage
1 cup a day, 1 tbsp at a time.
Recommendation: This tea can also be used to treat bronchial catarrh.

EUCALYPTUS

Eucalyptus globulus
Kapoora maram

Ingredients

Leaves, crushed	½ tsp
Boiling water	½ cup

Method
Infuse the eucalyptus leaves in boiling water for 5-10 minutes, keeping the pan covered, then strain and drink fresh. *Preparation time*: 5-10 *minutes.*

Dosage
½ cup, 3 times a day, freshly prepared.

FENUGREEK

Trigonella foenum-graecum Linn.
Methi

Ingredients

Seeds, crushed	1 tbsp
Water	4 cups

Method
Put the crushed seeds and water in a suitable container, cover and simmer gently for 30 minutes. Cool to room temperature and strain. *Preparation time: 30 minutes.*

Dosage
1 cup, 4 times a day.

HOLY BASIL

Ocimum sanctum
Tulsi

Ingredients

Leaves, ground	1 tbsp
Water	2 cups

Method
To make the tea, boil the ground leaves in the water for about 15 minutes or till only half the original volume is left. Strain the concentrate through a suitable strainer, cool and drink. *Preparation time: 15 minutes.*

Dosage
2 tbsp, 4 times a day.

LIQUORICE

Glycyrrhiza glabra
Mulethi

Ingredients

Liquorice, pulverised	1 tsp
Boiling water	1 cup

Method
Add the boiling water to the pulverised liquorice and let the mixture steep for 5 minutes in a covered container. Strain the tea before drinking. *Preparation time: 5 minutes.*

Dosage
1 cup, 3 times a day after meals.

Bronchial Catarrh

When too much mucus is produced in the respiratory system, it causes catarrh. If the mucus is produced in the lower respiratory tract, it causes bronchial catarrh.

ANISEED

Pimpinella anisum
Vilayati saunf

Ingredients

Seeds, crushed	1 tbsp
Water	2 cups

Method
Raise the mixture to a boil in a covered pan, cool, strain and drink. *Preparation time: 1 minute.*

Dosage
1 cup, twice a day.

PINE

Pinus sylvestris Linn.
Chir

Ingredients

Dried young shoots	1 tbsp
Water	1 cup

Method
Macerate the herb in cold water, then bring the mixture to a boil. Remove from the heat and let it stand covered for 15 minutes. Strain before drinking.
Preparation time: boiling time 1–2 minutes; standing time 15 minutes.

Dosage
½ cup, twice a day.

Burns are caused by dry heat from fire or other sources such as electricity, friction and chemicals. Scalds are caused by boiling liquids or steam.

In superficial or first degree burns, only the outer layers of the skin are damaged. In such burns and scalds the skin becomes red and there may be some pain.

In second degree burns, the skin looks scorched, blackened and blistered, and the burned or scalded area is painful.

In severe or third degree burns, all the layers of the skin are destroyed. The skin becomes dark red, charred or blistered. There is little or no pain because the nerve endings have been destroyed. The burn victim may develop the so-called 'burn shock'. In this condition, the liquid in the blood is sent by the body into the burned areas. There may not be enough blood volume left to keep the brain, heart and other organs functioning.

An excellent first aid for burns is to submerge the burned area in cold water (as cold as possible) within 25 minutes of the injury, for 10 to 15 minutes. This will soothe the inflammation and slow the swelling process.

Minor burns and scalds, if limited to a small skin area, may be considered for herbal treatment. For all other burns, immediate medical help should be sought.

MARIGOLD

Calendula officinalis
Zergul

Ingredients

Whole flower head, crushed	1–2 tsp
Boiling water	2 cups

Method

Place the herb in a pan, cover with the boiling water and steep for 15 minutes with the lid closed. Strain.

Preparation time: 15 minutes.

Dosage

1 cup a day.

Helpful hint: Honey hastens the healing process and is effective in curing thermal burns, particularly those that take a long time to heal. It may be ingested or applied locally.

STINGING NETTLE

Urtica dioica
Bichhu

Ingredients

Dried leaves, crushed	2 tsp
Water	1 cup

Method

Boil the mixture of nettle leaves and water for 5 minutes. Remove from the heat, cover the pan and allow the mixture to stand for 1 hour. Strain and drink. *Preparation time: boiling time 5 minutes; standing time 1 hour.*

Dosage

⅓ cup, 3 times a day.

The common cold is a contagious viral infection, occurring more often in cold weather but common enough all year round. During a viral attack the mucous membrane of the nose becomes inflamed inducing sneezing, and there is a constant flow of thin mucus. The nasal stuffiness resulting from the inflammation compromises normal breathing and interferes with sleep. A cold usually lasts about a week before subsiding by itself.

The causes of the common cold are viruses, low body resistance, excessive use of sour and cold things and inhalation of smoke and dust.

CINNAMON

Cinnamomum zeylanicum
Dalchini

Ingredients

Bark, powdered	3 g
Water	1½ cups

Method
Boil the cinnamon in the water for 15 minutes in a covered container. Strain the decoction and sweeten with sugar before drinking. *Preparation time: 15 minutes.*

Dosage
½ cup, twice a day.

DOG ROSE

Rosa canina

Ingredients

Dried rose hips, shredded	2 tsp
Water	2 cups

Method

Boil the herb in the water for 10 minutes, keeping the vessel covered throughout. Strain the mixture and drink twice a day. *Preparation time: 10 minutes.*

Dosage

1 cup, twice a day.

GINGER

Zingiber officinale Rosc.
Adrak

Ingredients

Rhizomes, shredded	30 g
Boiling water	2 cups

Method

Cover the rhizomes with boiling water, close the lid of the pan and let the mixture steep for 5-20 minutes, depending on the strength of the tea desired. Strain the infusion before drinking the liquid extract. *Preparation time: 5-20 minutes.*

Dosage

1-2 cups a day.

HOLY BASIL

Ocimum sanctum
Tulsi

Ingredients

Dried leaves, crushed	1 tsp
Water	2 cups

Method
Prepare the decoction by cooking the leaves in 2 cups water till only 1 cup of the liquid remains in the pan. Strain the mixture and discard the leaves. *Preparation time: 15 minutes.*

Dosage
2 tbsp, 4 times a day.

LIQUORICE

Glycyrrhiza glabra
Mulethi

Ingredients

Liquorice, powdered	1 tsp
Boiling water	½ cup

Method
Mix the powder in ½ cup boiling water and let the mixture stand for 5 minutes. Strain the infusion and drink after meals. *Preparation time: 5 minutes.*

Dosage
½ cup, 3 times a day after meals.

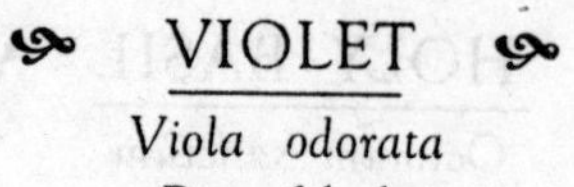

VIOLET

Viola odorata

Bunafshah

Ingredients

Fresh flowers, crushed	6 g
Water	1½ cups

Method

Add the flowers to the water and boil for 15 minutes, keeping the vessel covered. Strain the mixture and discard the flowers, retaining the liquid. *Preparation time: 15 minutes.*

Dosage

½ cup, twice a day.

More About Liquorice

The medicinal properties of this herb have been known to herbalists for thousands of years. The Greeks and Romans extracted its juice to quench their thirst. Practioners of traditional Chinese medicine prescribe it as a detoxificant and for digestive problems. Herbalists recommend its use as an immune tonic and believe that it has anti-inflammatory and antiulcer properties. It is a mild expectorant and is known to have some antiviral and antibacterial activity.

WORMWOOD

Artemisia absinthium
Vilayati afsanthin

Ingredients

Dried/fresh whole plant, chopped	1 tsp
Boiling water	1 cup

Method
Soak the herb in the water for 5-10 minutes, then strain and drink. *Preparation time: 5-10 minutes.*

Dosage
1 cup, 3 times a day.

JUJUBE + QUINCE + SEBESTAN

Ziziphus jujuba+ *Cydonia oblonga* + *Cordia dichotoma*
Unnab/Ber + Bihi + Sipistan/Lahora

Ingredients

Jujube fruit, crushed	5 numbers
Quince seeds, crushed	3 g
Sebestan fruit, crushed	9 numbers
Water	3½ cups

Method
Combine the jujube and sebestan fruit and boil in 1½ cups water for 15 minutes. Meanwhile, soak the quince seeds in the remaining ¼ cup water and extract the mucilage. Next, strain the decoction of jujube and sebestan and add the liquid extract to the mucilage of the quince seeds. Sweeten the mixture with honey before serving. *Preparation time: 15 minutes.*

Dosage
½ cup, 3 times a day.

Conjunctivitis

This disorder of the eye is caused by the inflammation of the mucous membrane, the conjunctiva, which lines the white part of the eye and the inner surface of the eyelids. The eye becomes red due to the dilation of the numerous blood vessels over the surface of the conjunctiva. Conjunctivitis is caused by exposure to chemicals in cosmetics, smoke, dust, the intense light in welding operations, allergy, or by infection, either viral or bacterial. It may also accompany a common cold or measles.

A symptom of conjuctivitis is an uncomfortable itching sensation in the eyes. If bacterial infection is present, a thick yellow discharge or pus collects in the corners of the eyes causing the eyelashes to stick together. They have to be bathed with warm water before the eyes can be opened.

EYEBRIGHT

Euphrasia officinalis

Dudhi

Ingredients

Dried herb, crushed	1 tbsp
Water	1 cup

Method

Stir the herb into the water and boil the mixture for 2 minutes. Remove the pan from the fire, cover and cool for 5-10 minutes before straining. *Preparation time: boiling time 2 minutes; standing time 5–10 minutes.*

Dosage

1 cup, 3 times a day.

Recommendation: This tea is especially useful for treating inflamed eyelids.

CHEBULIC MYROBALAN + EAST INDIAN GLOBE THISTLE + JUJUBE

Terminalia chebula + *Echinops indica* + *Ziziphus jujuba*
Halaila/Harad + Gorakmundi + Unnab/Ber

Ingredients

Chebulic myrobalan bark, ground	4 g
East Indian globe thistle, ground	6 g
Jujube fruit, ground	5 numbers
Water	1¾ cups

Method

Combine the herbs and boil them in 1¾ cups water in a covered vessel for 15 minutes. Remove from the heat and cool

More About Cinnamon

The bark of a tree that grows in Asia, cinnamon's medicinal use has been known for thousands of years. Indian herbalists recommend it for colds, fevers, and to treat diarrhoea. The ancient Egyptians used it in embalming, and a German herbalist, Hildegard, of the 12th century, called it a universal cure.

The inability to pass faecal matter is known as constipation. The faeces become dry, hard and pebbly, and thus difficult to pass. However, not emptying the bowels daily is not constipation. Normal bowels may empty two or three times a day or even every other day. The symptoms of persistent constipation are difficult or infrequent passing of motions, a feeling of heaviness in the body, headache, loss of appetite, flatulence and lethargy.

The causes of constipation are illness, eating very little amounts of food, sedentary habits, lack of exercise, and lack of roughage and fluids.

Herbal teas help in the bowel movement by softening the stool.

CHEBULIC MYROBALAN

Terminalia chebula
Harad/Halaila

Ingredients

Fruits, crushed	6 numbers
Water	1¼ cups

Method
Prepare the decoction by boiling the herb together with 3g. cinnamon for 10 minutes in a covered pan. Strain and drink in the morning. *Preparation time: 10 minutes.*

Dosage
½ cup, once a day.

FENNEL

Foeniculum vulgare Hill
Saunf

Ingredients

Seeds, crushed	1 tsp
Water	½ cup

Method
Soak the crushed fennel seeds in the water for 30 minutes, keeping the container covered. Strain the fennel tea and drink. *Preparation time: 30 minutes.*

Dosage
1 tsp, twice a day.

PURGING CASSIA

Cassia fistula
Amaltas

Ingredients

Pulp of ripe pod	12 g
Boiling water	½ cup

Method
Pour the boiling water over the pulp and allow the mixture to stand, uncovered, for 5-6 hours. Strain and drink at bedtime. *Preparation time: 5-6 hours.*

Dosage
1 tbsp at bedtime.

Constipation

SENNA

Cassia angustifolia
Senna

Ingredients

Leaves, crushed	1 tsp
Boiling water	1 cup

Method
Steep the leaves in the boiling water for 30 minutes, keeping the lid of the vessel closed. At the end of the steeping period strain the mixture and drink at bedtime.
Preparation time: 30 minutes.

Dosage
½ cup at bedtime.

FENNEL + LINSEED + LIQUORICE

Foeniculum vulgare Hill + *Linium usitatissimum* + *Glycyrrhiza glabra*
Saunf + Alsi + Mulethi

Ingredients

Fennel seeds, powdered	⅓ tsp
Linseed seeds, powdered	⅓ tsp
Liquorice root, powdered	⅓ tsp
Water	1¾ cups

Method
Combine equal quantities of the three herbs and add this herb mixture to the water and boil, covered, for 10 minutes. Filter the decoction before drinking. *Preparation time: 10 minutes.*

Dosage
1 cup, 3 times a day.

A cough is a condition in which air is expelled with a sudden opening of the glottis – the entrance to the windpipe – associated with a characteristic sound. It is a protective reflex by which phlegm and foreign particles are expelled from the air passages. The cough may have its origin in the inflammation of the larynx, which is the organ of voice, or the pharynx, which is the cavity at the back of mouth.

The common causes of a cough are the common cold, respiratory infection and mucus in the pharynx.

ANISEED

Pimpinella anisum

Vilayati saunf

Ingredients

Seeds, crushed	1–2 tsp
Boiling water	1 cup

Method

To prepare aniseed tea, place the crushed seeds in a pan and pour over the boiling water. Cover the pan and allow the tea to stand for 15 minutes. Strain and drink hot.

Preparation time: 15 minutes.

Dosage

1 cup, 2-3 times a day.

CATNIP

Nepeta cataria
Guli gaozaban

Ingredients

Dried leaves and flowering tops, ground	14 g
Boiling water	2 cups

Method
Pour the boiling water over the herb and steep for 5-10 minutes. Strain and drink at room temperature.
Preparation time: 5-10 minutes.

Dosage
1 cup on awakening and 1 cup at bedtime.

Caution: Not recommended for children under the age of two.

EUCALYPTUS

Eucalyptus globulus
Kapoora maram

Ingredients

Leaves, crushed	½ tsp
Boiling water	⅔ cup

Method
Steep the eucalyptus leaves in the boiling water for 20 minutes. Keep the pan covered during the steeping period. Strain and drink. *Preparation time: 20 minutes.*

Dosage
⅔ cup, 3 times a day.

HOREHOUND

Marrubium vulgare
Pahari gandana

Ingredients

Flowering tops, crushed	1 handful
Water	2 cups

Method
Boil the flowering tops of horehound in 2 cups water in a covered container for 15 minutes. Remove from the heat and allow the tea to stand for another 15 minutes. Strain the mixture and drink at room temperature. *Preparation time: boiling time 15 minutes; standing time 15 minutes.*

Dosage
1 cup a day, 1 tbsp at a time.

LINSEED

Linium usitatissium
Alsi

Ingredients

Seeds, crushed	15 g
Boiling water	2 cups

Method
Pour the boiling water over the crushed seeds, cover the container and let the tea steep for 5-20 minutes. Strain and drink hot or warm. *Preparation time: 5-20 minutes.*

Dosage
1-2 cups a day.

MALABAR NUT

Adhatoda vasika Nees.
Adosa

Ingredients

Leaves, crushed	7 numbers
Boiling water	1 cup

Method

Steep the crushed leaves in boiling water for 15 minutes in a covered container and strain. *Preparation time: 15 minutes.*

Dosage

1-4 tbsp, 4 times a day.

VIOLET

Viola odorata
Bunafshah

Ingredients

Dried flowers, chopped	1-2 tsp
Boiling water	2 cups

Method

Mix the flowers with the boiling water and let the mixture stand for 5-7 minutes. Filter the watery extract and drink while it is still warm. *Preparation time: 5-7 minutes.*

Dosage

1 cup, 3 times a day.

YARROW

Achillea millefolium
Gandana

Ingredients

Dried flowering plant, crushed	2-3 tsp
Cold water	4 cups

Method
Infuse the crushed plant in the cold water and allow the mixture to stand for 6-8 hours. Strain before drinking.
Preparation time: 6-8 hours.

Dosage
1 cup, 4 times a day.

COLTSFOOT + COMFREY + MARSHMALLOW + SAGE

Tussilago farafra + Symphytum offcinale + Althea officinalis + Slvia officinalis
Watapana + Khatmi + Salvia/Sefakuss

Ingredients

Coltsfoot leaves, powdered	¼ tsp
Comfrey leaves, powdered	¼ tsp
Marshmallow root, powdered	¼ tsp
Sage leaves, powdere5d	¼ tsp
Boiling water	2 cups

Method
Combine equal parts of the powdered herbs and pour the boiling water over the mixture. Let stand, covered, for 15 minutes and then strain the mixture. *Preparation time: 15 minutes.*

Dosage
1 cup, 3 times a day.

ANISEED + SUNDEW + THYME

Pimpinella anisum + Drosera rotundifolia + Thymus vulgaris, Linn.

Vilayati saunf + Muka jali + Ajwain

Ingredients

Aniseed, powdered	1/3 tsp
Sundew, whole plant, powderd	1/3 tsp
Thyme, whole plant, powdered	1/3 tsp
Boiling water	1 cup

Method

Combine the herbs and place in a container with a lid. Pour boiling water, cover and steep for 15 minutes. Strain and drink.

Preparation time: 15 minutes.

Dosage

1 cup, 3 times a day.

LIQUORICE + POPPY

Glycyrrhiza glabra + Papavar somniferum

Mulethi + Khas khas

Ingredients

Liquorice root, powdered	3 g
Poppy seeds, lightly crushed	2 g
Water	1 cup

Method

Combine the lightly crushed poppy seeds with the powdered liquorice and place in a container. Pour 1 cup water over the mixture, bring to a simmer and remove from the heat. Let the tea stand, covered, for 10 minutes before straining.

Preparation time: 10 minutes.

Dosage

1 cup, 3 times a day.

Whooping cough, or pertussis, is a childhood disease. Its onset is marked by a runny nose, watery eyes, irritation of the throat, sneezing, excessive coughing, which becomes worse at night, and fever. As the cough becomes more violent and its frequency and duration increase, the lungs are deprived of air. The face of the child turns red, the tongue protrudes from the mouth, there is perspiration on the face, followed by a sudden rush of air into the lungs attended with a high-pitched sound, the characteristic whoop. This condition is often followed by vomiting, particularly if the attack occurs after a meal. One attack gives immunity for life. Adults do not contract this disease.

MARJORAM

Origanum majorana L.
Marwa

Ingredients

Marjoram, chopped	2 tsp
Boiling water	2 cups

Method
Combine the boiling water and the herb in a container, cover and let the mixture stand for 15 minutes. Strain the tea and drink at room temperature. *Preparation time: 15 minutes.*

Dosage
1 cup, twice a day.

Cough, Whooping

MULLEIN

Verbascum thapsus Linn.
Gidar tamaku

Ingredients

Dried blossoms, crushed	1-2 tsp
Boiling water	1 cup

Method

Add the blossoms to the boiling water, cover the pan and steep for 10 minutes. Strain the tea before drinking. *Preparation time: 10 minutes.*

Dosage

1 cup, 2-3 times a day.

THYME

Thymus vulgaris Linn.
Ajwain

Ingredients

Leaves, tops, chopped	2 tsp
Boiling water	1 cup

Method

Steep the herb in the boiling water for 10 minutes in a covered vessel, then strain. *Preparation time: 10 minutes.*

Dosage

1 cup, 3-4 times a day.

Recommendation: Thyme tea is also recommended for spasmodic or dry coughs.

THYME + SUNDEW

Thymus vulgaris Linn. + *Drosera rotundifolia*
Ajwain + Muka jali

Ingredients

Thyme leaves, ground	2/3 tsp
Sundew, whole plant, ground	1/3 tsp
Boiling water	1 cup

Method
Place the herbs in a container with a lid. Add the boiling water, cover and steep for 10-15 minutes. Strain the mixture, bring to room temperature and drink.
Preparation time: 10–15 minutes.

Dosage
1 cup, 2-3 times a day.

More About Eucalyptus

The leaf of this tree is the sole food of the Australian koala bear. The aborignes of Australia used it as a remedy for coughs, fever and asthma. The Europeans believed that it could also cure malaria and so it came to be known as the Australian fever tree, but this belief was misplaced. However, the oil of the eucalyptus leaf contains eucalyptol, which is an excellent decongestant and also kills some types of viruses and bacteria.

The inflammation of the lining of the bladder caused by a bacterial infection is known as cystitis. Women are more prone to this disorder than men, because bacteria can gain easy access to the bladder due to the short length of the urethra, the channel through which urine is passed.

The symptoms of cystitis are bladder irritation, pain and a burning sensation on passing urine. Urine is passed more often than normal and sometimes there is blood in the urine due to the irritation of the bladder walls. The infection may spread to the kidneys causing back pain and fever.

Urine retention, prostate gland enlargement and constipation can lead to the bladder becoming infected.

BEARBERRY

Arctostaphylos uva-ursi

Ingredients

Dried leaves, coarsely powdered	1-2 tsp
Water	1 cup

Method

Pour the water over the powdered leaves, cover the vessel and leave for 6-12 hours. Do not heat or boil the leaves as this will make them bitter and destroy their efficacy. Strain the liquid and drink it cold. *Preparation time: 6-12 hours.*

Dosage

1 cup, twice a day.

Caution: During the course of this treatment, the urine may turn a sharp green colour – a harmless side effect. Long–term use of this tea is not recommended as its high tannin content may result in constipation and an upset stomach.

BIRCH

Betula pendula/B. pubescens

Bojpatra

Ingredients

Fresh/dried leaves, crushed	1 tsp
Boiling water	1 cup

Method

Drop the birch leaves into the water, cover and let the leaves steep in the water for 5-10 minutes. Strain the infusion, discard the leaves and drink the watery extract.

Preparation time: 5–10 minutes.

Dosage

1 cup, 3 times a day.

JUNIPER

Juniperus communis

Abbhal/Aaraar

Ingredients

Berries, lightly crushed	1 tsp
Boiling water	1 cup

Method

Soak the berries in the boiling water for 20 minutes, taking care to keep the vessel covered. Then strain, discard the berries and drink the liquid morning and evening.

Preparation time: 20 minutes.

Dosage

1 cup, twice a day.

Caution: This tea is not recommended for pregnant women and those suffering from inflammation of the kidneys.

Diabetes

This condition occurs when the body cannot properly utilise sugar, or glucose, and carbohydrates from the diet because the pancreas fails to produce sufficient quantities of insulin. Insulin plays an important role in transporting sugar through the bloodstream into the body tissues, where it is needed for the production of energy. Diabetes is sometimes referred to as a metabolic disturbance, in which the process of storage and expenditure of nutrition is disturbed so that the glucose, instead of being stored in the liver and muscles, and used when required, is excreted in the urine. This insulin deficiency leads to serious complications, namely, the impairment of eyesight and mental sharpness, culminating in a 'diabetic coma', followed by death.

The symptoms of diabetes include excessive appetite, frequent passage of large amounts of urine (polyuria) which may contain glucose (Diabetes mellitus), or from which glucose is absent (Diabetes insipidus, a rare disorder), excessive thirst, skin eruptions associated with itching, visual changes and cataracts, lowered resistance to infection, lethargy and loss of weight.

The various causes for the failure of the pancreas to produce sufficient insulin thus leading to diabetes, are inherited predisposition, consistent overeating, too much alcohol, a sedentary lifestyle, diseases of the liver and goitre, sudden emotional disturbances or shock, constant mental activity and serious injury to the head or the nervous system.

During pregnancy, there may be a transient onset of diabetes, but the condition returns to normal after childbirth.

BABUL

Acacia nilotica
Kikar

Ingredients

Bark, shredded	2 tbsp
Water	2 cups

Method
Steep the bark in 2 cups water for 12 hours. Keep the lid of the container closed. Strain and drink the liquid.
Preparation time: 12 hours.

Dosage
3-4 tbsp, twice a day.

JAMBOL

Eugenia jambolana
Jamun

Ingredients

Seeds, crushed	1 tsp
Water	1 cup

Method
Soak the seeds in the water for 8 hours, then strain.
Preparation time: 8 hours.

Dosage
1 tbsp, 3 times a day.

COTTON SEED

Gossypium herbaceum
Binola

Ingredients

Seeds, crushed	1 tsp
Water	3 cups

Method
Boil the cotton seeds in a covered container till the volume of the water is reduced to 1 cup. Strain the mixture and drink twice a day. *Preparation time: 30 minutes.*

Dosage
1 cup, twice a day

Caution: Cotton seed tea is not recommended for pregnant women.

DANDELION

Taraxacum officinale Weber
Kukraundha

Ingredients

Root, shredded	1-2 tsp
Water	1 cup

Method
Heat the mixture of root and water and boil for 2-3 minutes. Then remove from the fire and let it stand covered for 15 minutes before straining. *Preparation time: boiling time 2-3 minutes; standing time 15 minutes.*

Dosage
1 cup, morning and evening for 4-6 weeks.

FENUGREEK

Trigonella foenum-graecum Linn.
Methi

Ingredients

Seeds, crushed	1 tsp
Water	1 cup

Method

Soak the fenugreek seeds in the water, cover and leave overnight. Strain and drink the filtrate in the morning.
Preparation time: 8–10 hours.

Dosage

1 cup a day.

More About Fenugreek

The medicinal qualities of Fenugreek have been widely used in traditional system of healing, including Ayurveda. The leaves are high in protein content while seeds are rich in calcium, iron and vitamin C. The leaves are beneficial in treating flatulence, sluggish liver and mouth ulcers. The seeds are a rich source of fibre and their alkaloid content is known to reduce blood sugar level. Studies at the National Institute of Nutrition, Hyderabad, have confirmed improvement in glucose tolerance and decrease in cholesterol level with use of these seeds. The fenugreek seed powder can be easily mixed in rice, vegetables and bread.

MANGO

Magnifera indica Linn.
Aam

Ingredients

Leaves, chopped	8-10 numbers
Water	1 cup

Method
Place the leaves in a mortar, add the water and grind. Strain and drink. *Preparation time: 5 minutes.*

Dosage
1 cup a day for 20–25 days.

BAYBERRY + CHEBULIC MYROBALAN + LODH TREE + NUT GRASS

Myrica cerifera + Terminalia chebula + Symplocos racemosa + Cyperus rotundus

Kaiphala + Harad + Lodh + Nagarmotha

Ingredients

Bayberry bark, chopped	2 g
Chebulic myrobalan bark, finely chopped	2 g
Lodh tree bark, finely powdered	2 g
Nut grass tubercles, ground	2 g
Boiling water	1 cup

Method
Combine all the herbs in a pan and pour the boiling water over the mixture. Cover and let it stand for 15 minutes, stirring occasionally. Strain, and the tea is ready to drink. *Preparation time: 15 minutes.*

Dosage
1 cup, twice a day.

Diarrhoea

This is a common symptom of a wide range of conditions. It can be acute, lasting only a few days, or chronic and recurrent. The former is usually caused by food poisoning or a viral infection. The causes of the latter are usually more serious. Diarrhoea may be accompained by extreme thirst and dryness of the mouth and tongue. Severe diarrhoea causes a loss of fluids leading to dehydration.

Any of the following herbal teas may be taken to overcome the loss of both fluids and minerals during an attack of simple diarrhoea.

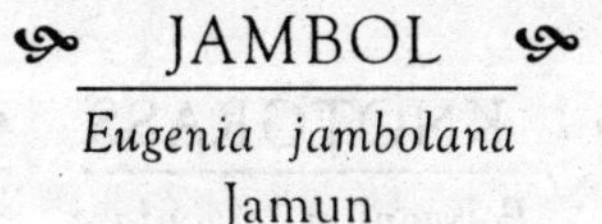

JAMBOL

Eugenia jambolana

Jamun

Ingredients

Root/leaves, crushed	1–2 tsp
Boiling water	1 cup

Method

Pour the boiling water over the root or leaves and steep in a covered pan for 10–15 minutes. Filter and drink the filtrate. *Preparation time: 10–15 minutes.*

Dosage

1 cup, 6 times a day.

BLACK PEPPER

Piper nigrum
Kali mirch

Ingredients

Seeds, crushed	5 numbers
Water	1 cup

Method
Boil the seeds in the water for 15 minutes in a covered container. Remove from the heat and strain.
Preparation time: 15 minutes.

Dosage
½ tsp, twice a day.

KNOTGRASS

Polygonum aviculare
Kumar

Ingredients

Flowering plant, freshly chopped	3–4 tsp
Water	2 cups

Method
Boil the knotgrass in 2 cups water for 15 minutes. Remove from the heat and set aside for another 15 minutes to cool. Then strain and drink as recommended.
Preparation time: boiling time 15 minutes; standing time 15 minutes.

Dosage
1 cup, twice a day.

MARJORAM

Origanum majorana L.
Marwa

Ingredients

Dried flowers, chopped	2 tsp
Boiling water	4 cups

Method
Add the boiling water to the dried flowers, cover and let the mixture stand for 10 minutes, then strain.
Preparation time: 10 minutes.

Dosage
1 cup, 4 times a day.

SPEARMINT

Mentha spicata Linn.
Pahadi pudina

Ingredients

Whole plant, crushed	1 tsp
Water	2 cups

Method
Raise the mixture of herb and water to a boil. After 5 minutes turn off the heat and let it stand covered for 10 minutes. Strain and drink. *Preparation time: boiling time 5 minutes; standing time 10 minutes.*

Dosage
1 cup, twice a day.
Recommendation: Spearmint tea is useful in treating diarrhoea caused by chills.

YARROW

Achillea millefolium Linn.
Gandana

Ingredients

Whole plant, chopped	2–3 tbsp
Water	4 cups

Method

Steep the chopped herb in 4 cups water for 5-6 hours, keeping the pan covered. Strain the extract before drinking. *Preparation time: 5–6 hours.*

Dosage

1 cup, 4 times a day.

CINNAMON + CLOVE + POMEGRANATE

Cinnamomum zeylanicum + *Eugenia caryophyllus* + *Punica granatum*
Dalchini + Laung + Anar

Ingredients

Cinnamon bark	1.25 cm
Cloves	2–3 numbers
Pomegranate bark and rind of fruit, crushed	1 tsp
Water	¾ cup

Method

Combine the pomegranate bark and fruit with the water and boil for 10 minutes in a covered container. Add the cloves and cinnamon for flavour and strain. *Preparation time: 10 minutes.*

Dosage

2-4 tsp, 4 times a day.

Medically, fever means higher than normal body temperature and may be accompanied by shivering, headache, body ache and other symptoms. Generally the temperature of a normal, healthy individual ranges between 98.4°F to 99.5°F (36.9°C to 37.5°C). Fever is a symptom of a variety of causes. The presence of fever suggests the body is fighting infection, dehydration, blood disease or malignancy.

The early stages of common fever can be best managed by taking any of the following herbal teas and extracts as they contain pharmaceutically active substances that fight the fever.

BLACK PEPPER

Piper nigrum

Kali mirch

Ingredients

Seeds, coarsely powdered	3–6 g
Water	2 cups

Method

Mix the pepper with the water and boil the mixture till the quantity of liquid is reduced to ¼ cup. Strain the decoction and sweeten with a little sugar. *Preparation time: 25 minutes.*

Dosage

¼ cup, twice a day.

Recommendation: Black pepper tea is an effective treatment for obstinate fevers.

CORIANDER

Coriandrum sativum

Dhania

Ingredients

Seeds, crushed	1 tsp
Boiling water	2 cups

Method

Add the coriander seeds to the boiling water, cover and steep for 15 minutes. Strain the infusion and drink several times a day. *Preparation time: 15 minutes.*

Dosage

¼ cup, 4 times a day.

GARLIC

Allium sativum

Lahsun

Ingredients

Pods, grated	10 g
Water	1½ cups
Milk	3 tbsp

Method

Combine the milk and water and add the garlic. Bring this mixture to a boil and continue cooking till the liquid is reduced to ¼ cup, then strain. *Preparation time: 15–20 minutes.*

Dosage

3 tbsp a day.

Recommendation: An excellent remedy for intermittent, remittent and malarial fevers.

HOLY BASIL

Ocimum sanctum
Tulsi

Ingredients

Dried leaves	11 g
Water	2 cups

Method
Heat the mixture of leaves and water and cook until only half of the original volume remains. Strain this concentrate and add milk, sugar and cardamom to improve the taste.
Preparation time: 15 minutes.

Dosage
¼-½ cup, twice a day.

Recommendation: Excellent for treating malarial and dengue fevers.

NEEM

Azadirachta indica
Neem

Ingredients

Bark, lightly pounded	30 g
Water	3 cups

Method
To prepare neem tea, boil the bark in 3 cups water for 15 minutes. Keep the container covered while boiling. Then remove from the fire and strain. Sweeten with a little sugar.
Preparation time: 15 minutes.

Dosage
4-8 tbsp, 3 times a day.

BLACK PEPPER + GARDEN QUININE

Piper nigrum + *Clerodendrum inerme*
Kali mirch + Kundali/Sung kupi

Ingredients

Black pepper seeds	5–10 numbers
Garden quinine leaves, fresh	15–30 numbers
Boiling water	1½ cups

Method
Drop the herbs in the water, cover and steep for 15 minutes. Then strain the tea, discard the herbs and sweeten the extract with a little sugar. *Preparation time: 15 minutes.*

Dosage
½ cup, 3 times a day. Reduce the dose for children.

GINGER + MINT

Zingiber officinale Rosc. + *Mentha arvensis*
Adrak + Pudina

Ingredients

Ginger rhizomes, crushed	2 g
Mint leaves, crushed	2 g
Water	1½ cups

Method
Mix the 2 herbs in the water and bring to a boil. Cover and cook for 15 minutes. Strain the decoction and drink.
Preparation time: 15 minutes.

Dosage
¼ cup, twice a day.

Recommendation: This tea is an efficient remedy for high fevers.

The wind or gas produced in the stomach or intestines is known as 'flatus'. Belching, passing wind (flatulence) and a bloated feeling are symptoms of gas in the digestive system. Often gas is produced by swallowing air while eating, or the cause may be foods that have not been broken down by the digestive juices and which then ferment in the bowel. Examples of foods that are difficult to digest are apples, beans, cauliflower, cucumber, melons, onions, radish, milk and eggs. Patients suffering from flatulence should restrict their intake of these foods and avoid hurry, worry, anxiety and tension during meals.

ANISEED

Pimpinela anisum Linn.
Vilayati saunf

Ingredients

Seeds, crushed	1-2 tsp
Boiling water	1 cup

Method

Put the boiling water and seeds in a covered container and let the tea infuse for 5-10 minutes. Discard the seeds by straining and drink the watery extract twice a day.

Preparation time: 5-10 minutes.

Dosage

1 cup, twice a day.

CARAWAY

Carum carvi
Siya zeera

Ingredients

Seeds, crushed	1 tsp
Boiling water	1 cup

Method
Place the crushed caraway seeds in the boiling water, cover the container and allow the mixture to steep for 15 minutes. Strain and drink. *Preparation time: 15 minutes.*

Dosage
1 cup, twice a day.

FENNEL

Foeniculum vulgare Mill
Saunf

Ingredients

Seeds, crushed	1-2 tsp
Boiling water	1 cup

Method
To prepare the fennel tea, pour the boiling water over the seeds, then steep the mixture, covered, for 5-10 minutes. Strain the infusion and drink 1-2 teaspoons at a time.
Preparation time: 5-10 minutes.

Dosage
1 cup, twice a day.

Caution: Not more than 1-2 tsp of this tea should be taken at a time.

PEPPERMINT

Mentha piperita
Paparaminta

Ingredients

Dried leaves, crushed	1 tsp
Boiling water	$^2/_3$ cup

Method

Infuse the crushed peppermint leaves in the boiling water for 5-10 minutes, depending on the strength of the tea required. Strain the infusion and drink between meals. *Preparation time: 5-10 minutes.*

Dosage

$^2/_3$ cup, 3-4 times a day, between meals.

SPEARMINT

Mentha spicata Linn.
Pahadi pudina

Ingredients

Dried leaves, crushed	1 tsp
Water	2 cups

Method

Raise the mixture of leaves and water to a boil, remove from the fire and let stand for 5-10 minutes. Strain and drink the extract between meals. *Preparation time: 5-10 minutes.*

Dosage

1 cup, 3-4 times a day.

CARAWAY + FENNEL + PEPPERMINT

Carum carvi + Foeniculum vulgare Mill + *Mentha piperita*
Siya zeera + Saunf + Paparaminta

Ingredients

Caraway seeds, powdered	2/3 tsp
Fennel seeds, powdered	2/3 tsp
Peppermint leaves, ground	2/3 tsp
Boiling water	1 cup

Method
Combine equal amounts of the herbs, pour boiling water over the mixture and let it stand for 5-10 minutes. Strain the tea and drink before meals. *Preparation time: 5–10 minutes.*

Dosage
1 cup, twice a day before meals, to be taken in small sips while still warm.

More About St John's Wort

When the leaves and flowers of this plant are pinched they release a red oil. Early Christians believed the plant released this blood-red oil on 29 August, the anniversary of the martyrdom of John the Baptist, and named it St John's wort in the saint's honour. In the Middle Ages, people kept the plant under the pillow or hung it over the door for protection against evil spirits. This herb is useful in treating menopausal neuroses and the oil is excellent for dry skin, especially in the elderly.

Gallstones are formed in the gall bladder and in the bile duct leading from the liver. Over time, there may be only one big-sized stone or as many as 200 tiny stones in the gall bladder; one of the tiny stones may find its way into the bile duct, thereby obstructing the flow of bile into the intestine. The result is pain with severe discomfort in the right upper part of the abdomen, accompanied by nausea, vomiting and flatulence. The pain may radiate to the back and right shoulder. Gallstones may result from a diet high in fat and from a chronic infection of the gall bladder.

Women past middle age are more likely than men to develop gallstones.

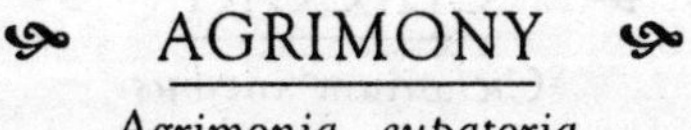

AGRIMONY

Agrimonia eupatoria
Khasi

Ingredients

Leaves, crushed	1 tsp
Boiling water	1 cup

Method
Drop the leaves into the boiling water, cover and steep for 10 minutes. Strain and drink as hot as possible in small sips. *Preparation time: 10 minutes.*

Dosage
1 cup, twice a day.

ARTICHOKE

Cynara scolymus

Hatichak

Ingredients

Dried leaves, crushed	1-2 tsp
Water	1 cup

Method

Add the leaves to the water, cover the pan and heat to boiling. Remove the pan from the fire and let the tea brew for 10 minutes before straining. *Preparation time: 10 minutes.*

Dosgae

1 cup, 2-3 times a day.

CHICORY

Cichorium intybus

Kasni

Ingredients

Root, flowers, seeds, crushed	2 tsp
Water	1 cup

Method

Pour the water over the herb, cover the container and steep for 10 minutes. Strain. *Preparation time: 10 minutes.*

Dosage

1 cup, twice a day.

DANDELION

Taraxacum officinale Weber

Kukraundha

Ingredients

Dried root, finely chopped	1-2 tsp
Water	2 cups

Method

Soften the root by soaking it in the water for 2 hours. Then heat the mixture and boil for 2 minutes. Remove from the fire and let it stand, covered, for 15 minutes and then strain.

Preparation time: boiling time 2 minutes; standing time 15 minutes.

Dosage

1 cup, twice a day.

GRAPES

Vitis vinifera

Angoor

Ingredients

Fresh/dried leaves, crushed	2-4 tsp
Water	1 cup

Method

Bring the mixture to a simmer, remove from the heat and leave it covered, for 15 minutes. Then strain and drink.

Preparation time: 15 minutes.

Dosage

1 cup, 3 times a day for several weeks.

Gums, Bleeding of

This disease is a result of vitamin C deficiency. The blood-carrying capillaries become fragile and subsequently rupture, allowing the blood to ooze out.

Gingivitis, a disease of the gums, also causes bleeding. Inadequate cleaning of the teeth results in the formation of plaque, a sticky film that coats the teeth and gums. This plaque hardens into tartar which destroys the fibres that connect the teeth to the gums. Gingivitis is characterised by bright pink gums which bleed when pressure is applied.

Sometimes bleeding gums may be a symptom of leukaemia.

ALPINE RAGWORT

Senecio fuchsil

Chitawala

Ingredients

Whole plant, chopped	1 tsp
Water	1 cup

Method

Heat the herb and water combination to a simmer, then remove from the fire, cover and let it stand for 15 minutes. Strain the tea before serving. *Preparation time: 15 minutes.*

Dosage

1 cup, 2-3 times a day.

Recommendation: This tea helps in stemming the bleeding after a tooth extraction.

STINGING NETTLE

Urtica dioica

Bichhu

Ingredients

Stalks, chopped	3-4 tsp
Boiling water	½ cup

Method

Pour the water over the nettle stalks, cover and set aside for 15 minutes, then strain. *Preparation time: 15 minutes.*

Dosage

½ cup, 3-4 times a day.

YARROW

Achillea millefolium

Gandana

Ingredients

Dried flowering plant, crushed	2-3 tbsp
Water	4 cups

Method

Let the yarrow stand in the water for 15 minutes in a covered container, then strain the infusion and drink the liquid as recommended. *Preparation time: 15 minutes.*

Dosage

1 cup, 4 times a day.

There are several types of headches, the most common being tension headaches, cluster headaches and migraines.

Tension Headache: It begins with a sensation of pain and tension, generally towards the back of the head. The pain rarely lasts for more than an hour but the feeling of tension may persist. It is caused by persistent contraction of the scalp muscles, which may be a result of prolonged concentration on a particular activity like reading or sewing. Also, emotional stress and anxiety can bring on a tension headache.

Cluster Headache: This type of headache causes severe pain and tends to occur nightly for several weeks or months and then may disappear for years. Unlike tension headaches, cluster headaches interfere with sleep. They start late at night with intense pain behind one eye, the eye fills with tears and the nose gets blocked on the affected side. There is rarely any nausea or vomiting. Cluster headaches are usually brought on by stress or alcohol.

Migraine: This is a type of recurrent headache confined to one side of the head only.The symptoms include nausea and vomiting, accompanied by visual distortions such as seeing 'stars' or an 'aura of spots' before the eyes, and a feeling of numbness or tingling in the face, a hand or a leg. A migraine occurs due to the sudden and inexplicable expansion and contraction of the arteries leading to one side of the head. Some foods may set off an attack of migraine. These include aged and strong cheese, pods of broad beans, canned figs and alcohol. Large amounts of monosodium glutamate employed as a flavouring agent in foods may also precipitate an attack of migraine.

꧁ BALM ꧂

Melissa officinalis
Rogani Balsan

Ingredients

Leaves, fresh/dried, crushed	2 tsp
Boiling water	1 cup

Method
Pour the boiling water over the leaves, cover the container and let the mixture stand for 10 minutes. Strain and sweeten with sugar or honey and drink hot. *Preparation time: 10 minutes.*

Dosage
1 cup twice a day.
Recommendation: Useful for tension headaches.

꧁ GINGER ꧂

Zingiber officinale
Adrak

Ingredients

Rhizomes, crushed	30 g
Boiling water	2 cups

Method
Combine the ginger and water in a covered pan and let it stand for 25 minutes. Then strain the infusion and drink hot or warm. *Preparation time: 25 minutes.*

Dosage
1-2 cups a day.
Recommendation: Ginger tea is an excellent remedy for migraines.

LAVENDER

Lavandula angustifolia
Dharu

Ingredients

Blossoms, crushed	1 tsp
Boiling water	1 cup

Method
Drop the blossoms into the boiling water, cover the vessel and allow the flowers to steep for 10-15 minutes, then strain. The tea is ready to drink. *Preparation time: 10–15 minutes.*

Dosage
1 cup, twice a day, morning and evening for 2-3 weeks.

ROSEMARY

Rosmarinus officinalis Linn.
Rusmary

Ingredients

Leaves crushed	1 handful
Water	2 cups

Method
In a covered container, boil the rosemary leaves in 2 cups water for 15 minutes, remove from the fire, cool and strain.
Preparation time: 15 minutes.

Dosage
1 cup, twice a day.
Recommendation: Rosemary tea brings relief from migraine headaches.

THYME-LEAVED GRATIOLA

Herpestis Moniera
Brhambhi

Ingredients

Leaves, crushed	½ tsp
Water	2 cups

Method
Boil the leaves in 2 cups water for 15 minutes in a covered container. Remove from the heat and allow the decoction to cool before straining it. *Preparation time: 15 minutes.*

Dosage
1–2 tbsp, twice a day.

VIOLET

Viola odorata
Bunafshah

Ingredients

Leaves, crushed	2 tsp
Boiling water	1 cup

Method
To 1 cup boiling water, add the crushed violet leaves and let the mixture stand, covered, for 15 minutes. Then strain and drink as recommended. *Preparation time: 15 minutes.*

Dosage
1 cup a day.

CHAMOMILE + LAVENDER + VALERIAN

Anthemis noblis + *Lavandula angustifolia* + *Valeriana officinalis* Linn.
Babunah + Dharu + Jalakan

Ingredients

Chamomile flowers, crushed	1 tsp
Lavender flowers, crushed	½ tsp
Valerian root, crushed	½ tsp
Boiling water	1 cup

Method
Place the herb mixture in 1 cup of boiling water, cover and steep for 8 hours. Strain and drink. *Preparation time: 8 hours.*

Dosage
1 cup, twice a day.

Caution: Pregnant and nursing women and children below two years of age should not drink this tea.

LEMON BALM + LIME + ROSEMARY

Melissa officinalis + *Citrus bergamia* Ris er Poi + *Rosmarinus officinalis* L.
Aspurk + Nimboo + Rusmary

Ingredients

Lemon balm herb, crushed	⅓ tsp
Lime flowers, crushed	⅓ tsp
Rosemary herb, crushed	⅓ tsp
Boiling water	1 cup

Method
Combine the three herbs and pour the boiling water over this mixture, cover and let the tea stand for 15 minutes, then strain. *Preparation time: 15 minutes.*

Dosage
1-4 cups a day.

Blood pumped by the heart through the arteries, veins and smaller vessels to every part of the body delivers oxygen and nutrients to the body's tissues and removes waste products.

The heartbeat or the pulse rate in an adult male is 70 to 72 times a minute and in a female, 78 to 82 times per minute. Diet is an important factor in maintaing a healthy heart, and smoking is known to be damaging to the heart and kidneys.

Some of the more common heart disorders are diseases of the heart and its blood vessels, like angina pectoris or chest pains caused by the reduction in the flow of blood to the coronary arteries which supply the heart muscle, and palpitations, which is an awareness of the heart beating in circumstances other than after exercise or anxiety.

CARDAMOM

Elettaria cardamomum Maton
Choti elaichi

Ingredients

Seeds, powdered	2 g
Assam tea leaves	½ tsp
Boiling water	2 cups

Method
Pour the boiling water over the tea leaves and let the mixture stand for 10 minutes. Strain the tea and add the powdered cardamom seeds to the filtrate. Stir and drink.
Preparation time: 10 minutes.

Dosage
1 cup, twice a day.

CASTOR OIL PLANT

Ricinus communis Linn.

Erandi

Ingredients

Root, shredded	90 g
Water	3 cups

Method

Make a decoction by boiling the root of the castor oil plant in 3 cups water in a covered container for 15 minutes. Add a little potassium carbonate to the mixture. Remove the container from the fire and let it stand for 15 minutes before straining. *Preparation time: boiling time 15 minutes; standing time 15 minutes.*

Dosage

1 cup, 3 times a day.

EPHEDRA

Ephedra vulgaris

Asmania

Ingredients

Branches, chopped	15 g
Boiling water	2 cups

Method

Put the chopped ephedra branches in the boiling water, cover the container and let the mixture steep for 5-20 minutes. Strain the tea and drink it hot or warm.
Preparation time: 5-20 minutes.

Dosage

1-2 cups of hot or warm tea a day.

GARLIC

Allium staivum Linn.
Lahsun

Ingredients

Garlic cloves, pulverised	10 g
Water	½ cup
Milk	½ cup

Method
Combine all three ingredients in a covered pan and bring to a simmer. Continue to cook gently until only half the liquid remains. Strain and cool the decoction before drinking.
Preparation time: 7–8 minutes.

Dosage
½ cup a day.

LAVENDER

Lavandula angustifolia
Dharu

Ingredients

Blossoms, crushed	1 tsp
Boiling water	1 cup

Method
Drop the blossoms into the boiling water, cover the container and let the flowers steep for 10 minutes. Strain the infusion, discarding the blossoms. The tea is now ready.
Preparation time: 10 minutes.

Dosage
1 cup, twice a day.

Heart Disorders

VALERIAN

Valeriana officinalis

Jalakan

Ingredients

Root, shredded	2 tsp
Water	1 cup

Method

Add the shredded root to the water and let the mixture stand, covered, for 8 hours. At the end of the 8 hours strain the infusion and warm lightly before drinking.

Preparation time: 8 hours.

Dosage

1 cup a day.

Caution: Valerian tea is not recommended for pregnant and nursing women.

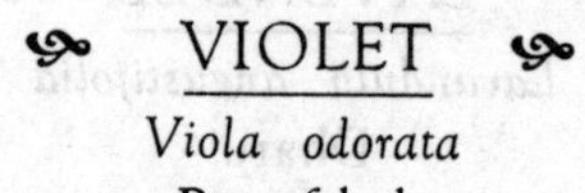

VIOLET

Viola odorata

Bunafshah

Ingredients

Flowers, crushed	15 g
Boiling water	2 cups

Method

Pour the boiling water over the crushed flowers, cover the container and let the mixture steep for 5-20 minutes. Strain the infusion and discard the flowers.

Preparation time: 5-20 minutes.

Dosage

1-2 cups a day.

Recommendation: Violet tea strengthens the heart and relieves angina pains.

Impotence is the failure to achieve and maintain satisfactory penile erection during the sex act. The failure to perform may cause anxiety and fear, sometimes leading to panic. This is called 'performance anxiety'. This type of male dysfunction is only transitory, more a psychological than a physical problem, and much of the treatment is self-help in nature. The first line of treatment, therefore, is reassurance and confidence that one is sexually potent.

Here are some teas that should help to allay the fears of sexual failure.

CORIANDER

Coriandrum sativum Linn.

Dhania

Ingredients

Leaves, chopped	1 tsp
Boiling water	1 cup

Method

To make the infusion, cover the coraindder leaves with boiling water, close the lid of the pan and leave for 15 minutes, then strain. *Preparation time: 15 minutes.*

Dosage

2-4 tbsp a day.

Helpful hint: The extract of coriander leaves acts as an aphrodisiac, while that of coriander seeds suppresses the sexual urge.

MARKING NUT

Semecarpus anacardium
Bhilava

Ingredients

Herb, crushed	1 tbsp
Water	½ cup

Method
Boil the herb till only half the liquid remains in the pan, then strain the extract and discard the herb.
Preparation time: 3–4 minutes.

Dosage
4 tbsp a day.

PEEPAL

Ficus religiosa
Peepal

Ingredients

Fruit, root, bark or tender shoots, crushed	1 tsp
Milk	1 cup

Method
Put the crushed herb in the milk and boil for 10 minutes. Strain and add sugar or honey to the tea. *Preparation time: 10 minutes.*

Dosage
¼ cup at bedtime.

Indigestion (Gastritis, Gastroenteritis)

Any minor discomfort in the stomach after meals is called indigestion.

The symptoms of indigestion are nausea, vomiting, belching, a foul smell in the mouth, heartburn, a feeling of fullness and pain or discomfort in the stomach, acidity, intestinal gases, constipation, diarrhoea and hiccups.

When food is not chewed thoroughly, the stomach secretes more acid than normal for its digestion. This extra acid, in combination with air which enters the stomach due to hurried chewing, is a source of irritation to the mucous lining of the stomach.

When food is introduced into the stomach, it causes its distension, and this in turn stimulates the churning activity in the stomach. However, when excessive distension takes place as a result of a heavy meal, the churning capability is inhibited, and this causes nausea and a feeling of fullness.

Fatigue, body ache and emotional upsets like depression or fear slow down the digestive activity of the stomach. Smoking also delays digestion, which results in the purtrefaction of food particles in the bowel, giving rise to flatulence.

Acute indigestion, also known as gastritis, acid stomach, dyspepsia and heartburn, occurs when the mucous membrane lining of the stomach becomes inflamed, resulting in a burning sensation in the upper abdomen and chest. Gastritis is caused by anxiety, nervous tension, overeating, allergy-causing foods like eggs, milk and fish, contaminated food and alcohol.

Gastroenteritis is the medical name for food poisoning. In this condition, the lining of the stomach and intestines becomes inflamed. The symptoms include vomiting, diarrhoea, abdominal cramps, temperature and perspiration.

ANISEED

Pimpinella anisum Linn.
Vilayati saunf

Ingredients

Seeds, crushed	1 tsp
Boiling water	1 cup

Method

Pour the boiling water over the crushed seeds and let the tea steep for 3-5 minutes. Strain and drink cold.
Preparation time: 3-5 minutes.

Dosage

1-2 cups a day, 1 tbsp at a time.

BELERIC MYROBALAN

Terminalia belerica
Bahera

Ingredients

Fruit pulp	1-3 g
Water	2 cups

Method

In a suitable vessel, boil the pulp in the water for 15 minutes. Strain the extract, discard the fruit, and the tea is ready.
Preparation time: 15 minutes.

Dosage

1 cup, twice a day.

Indigestion (Gastritis, Gastroenteritis)

CHEBULIC MYROBALAN

Terminalia chebula
Harad/Halaila

Ingredients

Powdered herb	3-12 g
Water	1 cup

Method
Mix together the herb and water. Do not boil or heat the tea but prepare at room temperature. *Preparation time: 5 minutes.*

Dosage
1 cup, twice a day.

CUMIN

Cuminum cyminum Linn.
Safed zeera

Ingredients

Seeds, crushed	1 tsp
Water	2 cups

Method
Add the crushed seeds to the water, cover the pan and let the mixture boil for 15 minutes. Strain and drink hot or warm. *Preparation time: 15 minutes.*

Dosage
1-2 cups a day.

GINGER

Zingiber officinale Rosc.
Adrak

Ingredients

Rhizomes, shredded	30 g
Boiling water	2 cups

Method

Steep the shredded herb in the boiling water for 5-20 minutes in a covered container. Strain the infusion and drink once or twice a day. *Preparation time: 5–20 minutes.*

Dosage

1 cup, twice a day.

SPEARMINT

Mentha spicata
Pahadi pudina

Ingredients

Leaves, crushed	1 tsp
Water	2 cups

Method

Put the leaves in the water, cover and bring the mixture to a boil. Continue boiling for 15 minutes, then remove from the heat, strain and drink while the tea is still warm.
Preparation time: 15 minutes.

Dosage

1 cup, twice a day.

Indigestion (Gastritis, Gastroenteritis)

CARDAMOM + CORIANDER

Elettaria cardamomum + *Coriandrum sativum*
Choti elaichi + Dhania

Ingredients

Cardamom seeds, powdered	11 g
Coriander seeds, powdered	60 g
Water	3 cups

Method
Combine all the ingredients, cover the pan and bring to a simmer. Continue cooking till the water is reduced to ½ cup. Strain before drinking. *Preparation time: 35 minutes.*

Dosage
Adults: 3-4 tbsp, 3 times a day.
Children: ¾-3 tsp, 3 times a day.

More About Coriander

Scheherazade, the mythical Arabian princess, in her stories, which later came to be known as *The Thousand and One Arabian Nights*, described coriander as an aphrodisiac. For thousands of years it was used as a digestive aid, and the seeds have even been found in the tombs of Egyptian pharaohs. The Bible tells us that when the Hebrews fled Egypt and slavery and were wandering in the desert, God fed them 'manna' from heaven, which was 'like coriander.' The Romans used both the seeds and the leaves of the plant as a meat preservative. The herb is an antioxidant and keeps animal fat from becoming rancid.

Difficulty in falling or staying asleep or waking up frequently in the night is called insomnia or sleeplessness. The most common causes for poor sleeping are worry, grief, an uncomfortable environment as, for example, excessive noise or a light or uncomfortable mattress. Drinking strong coffee or tea late at night can produce sleeplessness in people susceptible to caffeine.

Chronic sleeplessness can have serious consequences such as lack of energy, difficulty in concentration and irritability.

CALIFORNIA POPPY

Papaver californica Linn.

Ingredients

Flowering plant, crushed	1-2 tsp
Boiling water	1 cup

Method

Steep the herb in the boiling water for 10 minutes in a covered container. Strain the infusion and drink the liquid, morning and evening. *Preparation time: 10 minutes.*

Dosage

1 cup, twice a day, morning and evening for several weeks.

HOPS

Humulus lupulus Linn.

Ingredients

Whole plant, crushed	1 tsp
Boiling water	1 cup

Method

Let the hops soak in the boiling water for 15 minutes in a covered pan. Strain and drink in the evening. *Preparation time: 15 minutes.*

Dosage

1 cup in the evening.

MULLEIN

Verbascum thapsus Linn.

Gidar tamaku

Ingredients

Flowers, crushed	1–2 tsp
Boiling water	4 cups

Method

Add the mullein flowers to the boiling water, cover the vessel and let the mixture stand for 20 minutes. Strain, and the tea is ready. *Preparation time: 20 minutes.*

Dosage

1 cup, 4 times a day.

VALERIAN

Valeriana officinalis Linn.
Jalakan

Ingredients

Fresh root, shredded	2 tsp
Water	1 cup

Method
Soak the shredded valerian root in the water for 8 hours in a covered container, then gently warm the mixture, filter and drink the filtrate in the evening. *Preparation time: 8 hours.*

Dosage
1 cup in the evening.

Caution: This tea is not recommended for pregnant and nursing women.

ALMOND + BITTER BOTTLEGOURD + POPPY

Prunus dulcis + *Lagenaria siceraria* + *Papaver somniferum*
Badam + Kashiphala + Khas khas

Ingredients

Almonds	1.5 g
Bitter bottlegourd	1.5 g
Poppy seeds	3 g
Boiling water	1 cup

Method
Pulverise the first three ingredients to a powder in a mortar. Thoroughly stir the powder in the boiling water, then strain. Discard half the liquid and sweeten the remaining half with a little sugar and drink at bedtime. *Preparation time: 10 minutes.*

Dosage
½ cup at bedtime.

Billirubin is a yellow pigment which is produced when old red blood cells are broken down by the spleen. It is subsequently removed by the liver and discharged as bile, a greenish-yellow substance, into the intestines to aid digestion. When too much billirubin is produced in the blood, it results in jaundice. The excess yellow pigment imparts a yellow colour to the whites of the eyes, skin, sweat and urine.

Excess of yellow billirubin produced through liver damage following an infection is known as hepatitis. Haemolysis, caused by the excessive destruction of red blood cells, is seen in most normal babies shortly after birth. Obstructive jaundice occurs when the passage of the bile from the bile ducts into the intestines is obstructed by gallstones or cancer of the pancreas and bowel.

GOKULAKANTA

Hygrophila spinosa
Gokhulakanta

Ingredients

Root, finely chopped	1 tsp
Water	2 cups

Method
Boil the root for 20–30 minutes in a covered vessel, strain and take 2 or 3 times a day. *Preparation time:* 20–30 *minutes.*

Dosage
2-4 tbsp, 2-3 times a day.

MARIGOLD

Calendula officinalis Linn.
Zergul

Ingredients

Flowers, granulated	1–2 tsp
Boiling water	2 cups

Method
Place the flowers in a container and add the boiling water, cover and steep for 15 minutes. Then strain the liquid and take once a day. *Preparation time: 15 minutes.*

Dosage
1 cup a day.

NEEM

Azadirachta indica
Neem

Ingredients

Leaves, crushed	35 g
Water	½ cup
Honey	12 g

Method
Boil the neem in the water till the liquid has reduced by half. The vessel should be kept covered while it is on the fire. Then strain the concentrate, sweeten with honey and drink twice a day. *Preparation time: 3–4 minutes.*

Dosage
¼ cup, twice a day.

PEEPAL

Ficus religiosa

Peepal

Ingredients

Bark, powdered	1–4 g
Water	¼ cup

Method

Combine the peepal bark and the water in a pan, cover and heat to a simmer. Continue simmering till the liquid has reduced to half the original volume. Strain and take the extract in the morning. *Preparation time: 2–3 minutes.*

Dosage

1 tbsp a day.

PICRORHIZA

Picrorhiza kurroaa

Kutki

Ingredients

Seeds, powdered	1 tsp
Boiling water	1 cup

Method

Mix the powdered seeds in the boiling water, cover and leave for 10-15 minutes, then strain. *Preparation time: 10–15 minutes.*

Dosage

½ cup, twice a day.

WORMWOOD

Artemisia absinthium
Vilayati afsanthin

Ingredients

Fresh/dried whole plant, ground	1 tsp
Boiling water	1 cup

Method
In a covered vessel, combine the herb and the water and let the mixture stand for 10-15 minutes, strain and drink after meals. *Preparation time: 10–15 minutes.*

Dosage
1 cup, 3 times a day after meals.

FENNEL + MINT + ROSE

Foeniculum vulgare Linn. + *Mentha arvensis* + *Rosa damascena*
Saunf + Pudina + Gulab

Ingredients

Fennel seeds, crushed	6 g
Mint leaves, crushed	6 g
Rose flowers, crushed	6 g
Water	¾ cup

Method
Combine the herbs and boil them in ¾ cup water. Remove from the heat, cover and cool to room temperature, about 15-20 minutes. Drink the strained decoction twice a day. *Preparation time: 15–20 minutes.*

Dosage
¾ cup, twice a day.

Stones in the urinary tract may be formed by the crystallisation in the urine of excess salts present in the bloodstream, and can be caused by gout or hormone disorders. They may also result from an infection of the urinary tract, especially if the infection obstructs the flow of urine.

Kidney and bladder stones vary in size. Some may grow to a very large size, but go undetected as long as they stay in place. However, even a small stone can cause excruciating pain if it leaves the kidney and tears the lining of the urinary tract on its way to the bladder.

The symptoms of kidney and bladder stones are pain in the back of one kidney, which spreads to the groin area, pain on passing urine and blood in the urine.

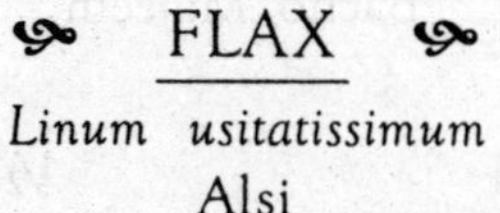

FLAX

Linum usitatissimum

Alsi

Ingredients

Seeds, crushed	15 g
Boiling water	2 cups

Method

Pour the boiling water over the seeds, cover the container and let the seeds soak in the water for 5 minutes for light tea and 20 minutes for stronger tea. Strain the tea before drinking.
Preparation time: 5–20 minutes.

Dosage

1-2 cups a day.

JUNIPER

Juniperus communis
Abbhal/Aarar

Ingredients

Fresh, ripe berries, crushed	1–2 tsp
Boiling water	1 cup

Method

Steep the berries in the boiling water for 2 minutes only, then strain. *Preparation time: 15 minutes.*

Dosage

¼–½ cup a day.

MADDER

Rubia tinctorum Linn.
Bacho/Majeeth

Ingredients

Root, shredded	½–2 tsp
Water	1 cup

Method

Soak the shredded madder root in 1 cup water for 8 hours in a covered container. Remove the root from the water by straining, and drink the remaining liquid twice a day. *Preparation time: 8 hours.*

Dosage

1 cup, twice a day.

Side effects: Madder tea may turn the urine red. This is a harmless side effect.

PARSELY

Petroselinum crispum
Prajmoda

Ingredients

Fruit, crushed	1 tsp
Boiling water	1¼ cups

Method
Combine the crushed fruit with the water, cover and let stand for 15 minutes, then strain. *Preparation time: 15 minutes.*

Dosage
3 tbsp a day.

Caution: Pregnant and nursing women should not take this tea.

RUPTUREWORT

Herniaria glabra

Ingredients

Dried/fresh herb, crushed	1 tsp
Boiling water	1 cup

Method
Add the herb to the boiling water, cover the pan and let the mixture stand for 30 minutes. Strain the infusion before drinking. *Preparation time: 30 minutes.*

Dosage
1 cup, 3 times a day.

VIOLET

Viola odorata
Bunafshah

Ingredients

Leaves, crushed	2 tsp
Water	1 cup

Method
Pour the water over the crushed leaves, cover the container and let the mixture stand for 24 hours. Strain the infusion and discard the leaves. *Preparation time: 24 hours.*

Dosage
1 cup, twice a day.

HORSEGRAM + RADISH

Dolichos biforus, Linn. + *Raphanus sativus, Linn.*
Kulthi + Mooli

Ingredients

Horsegram	6 g
Radish, grated	1½ tbsp
Water	½ cup

Method
Boil the horsegram in ½ cup water for 2-3 minutes, remove from the heat and strain. Then squeeze the water from the grated radish and add the extract to the tea.
Preparation time: 15 minutes.

Dosage
½ cup in the morning.

The internal secretions called hormones are responsible for the production of milk in a nursing mother. One such hormone is *prolactin*, which plays an essential role in the milk ejection reflex.

Mastitis or 'hard breasts' was always considered to be a result of poor flow of milk in nursing mothers.

Sometimes the breasts do not produce enough milk to satisfy the needs of the baby. Feeding the baby more frequently, say, every two hours, will increase the flow of milk because the suckling action promotes the release of the hormone prolactin.

Along with the herbal teas described below, which promote by an unknown mechanism the production of milk in women suffering from defective lactation, plenty of liquids, rest and a proper diet are also recommended.

ANISEED

Pimpenella anisum

Vilayati saunf

Ingredients

Seeds, crushed	1 tsp
Boiling water	1 cup

Method

Soak the seeds in 1 cup boiling water for 3-5 minutes, then strain. Allow the tea to cool completely before drinking.
Preparation time: 3–5 minutes.

Dosage

1 cup, twice a day, 1 tsp at a time.

BLACK CUMIN

Nigella sativa

Kala zeera

Ingredients

Seeds, crushed	1.5–3 g
Water	¼ cup

Method

Grind the seeds in ¼ cup water in a mortar, then strain the mixture and sweeten the liquid extract with honey.

Preparation time: 5 minutes.

Dosage

¼ cup a day.

NUT GRASS

Cyperus rotundus

Nagarmotha

Ingredients

Tubers, crushed	6 g
Water	4 cups

Method

Cook the tubers in 4 cups water for 15 minutes in a covered container. Strain the decoction and drink.

Preparation time: 15 minutes.

Dosage

1 cup 4 times a day.

ANISEED + CARAWAY + FENNEL

Pimpenella anisum + *Carum carvi* + *Foeniculum vulgare* Mill
Vilayati saunf + Siya zeera + Saunf

Ingredients

Aniseeds	¼–½ tsp
Caraway seeds	½–1 tsp
Fennel seeds	¼–½ tsp
Water	1 cup

Method
Combine the 3 herbs to make up 1-2 teaspoons of mixture, then lightly crush in a mortar. Add 1 cup water to the herb mixture and heat till the water begins to simmer. Remove from the heat and let the tea brew, covered, for a further 10 minutes. Strain before drinking. *Preparation time: 10 minutes.*

Dosage
1 cup a day.

ANISEED + FENUGREEK

Pimpenella anisum + *Trigonella foenum-graecum* Linn.
Vilayati saunf + Methi

Ingredients

Aniseeds, lightly crushed	¾ tsp
Fenugreek seeds, lightly crushed	1¼ tsp
Water	1 cup

Method
Bring the herb and water mixture to a simmer, then remove from the heat and set aside, covered, for 10 minutes. Strain and serve. *Preparation time: 10 minutes.*

Dosage
1 cup, 3 times a day

The inflammation of the larynx or voice box due to the common cold or infection in the respiratory tract is called laryngitis. Other causes include inhalation of dust or irritant chemicals, overuse of the voice and excessive smoking.

Acute laryngitis, which is infectious, comes on suddenly and is short-lived. Chronic laryngitis lasts longer and may recur, especially in people who breathe through the mouth.

The most prominent symptom is an unnatural change in the voice. In extreme cases, hoarseness and the complete loss of voice may occur. In addition, the throat feels sore and dry, and fever may follow.

CARAWAY

Carum carvi
Siya zeera

Ingredients

Root, shredded	1–2 tsp
Water	1 cup

Method
Bring the shredded caraway root and the water to a simmer in a covered container, then let it stand for 15-20 minutes away from the heat. Strain, and the tea is ready to drink.
Preparation time: 15-20 minutes.

Dosage
1 cup, twice a day.

HEDGE MUSTARD

Sisymbrium officinale

Khaksi

Ingredients

Whole plant, chopped	2 tsp
Boiling water	½ cup

Method

Combine the herb and water, cover the container and allow the mixture to stand for 20 minutes before straining.
Preparation time: 20 minutes.

Dosage

½ cup, twice a day.

LINSEED

Linum usitatissimum

Alsi

Ingredients

Seeds, crushed	12 g
Water	1 cup

Method

Mix the crushed seeds with water and boil this mixture till the liquid is reduced to half of the original volume. Strain the tea and add a little honey to it. *Preparation time: 7–8 minutes.*

Dosage

1 cup, twice a day.

WILD GINGER

Asarum canadense

Taggar

Ingredients

Root, shredded	1 tsp
Water	1 cup

Method

Put the ingredients in a covered container and gently bring to a simmer. Remove from the heat and let the mixture stand for 15 minutes. Strain and drink at room temperature.

Preparation time: 15 minutes.

Dosage

1 cup, twice a day.

More About Linseed/Flax

In Egypt and the Middle East the leaves of the linseed plant were once used to make linen. The ancient Egyptians and native Americans valued it for its nourishing and healing properties. Many herbalists still use it as a healing poultice. Its antioxidant properties help to improve overall health. Linseed oils are rich in omega-3 fatty acid, necessary for physical health. Fresh, unrefined linseed oil contains lecithin and other phospholipids which help to break down the oils and fats in the body, thus aiding digestion.

Leucorrhoea is characterised by a white, viscous and thick discharge from the vagina, resembling the white of an egg. It is a normal occurrence and usually does not point to any disorder. It may increase after menstruation. However, if the discharge is excessive and yellow or greenish in colour and has an unpleasant smell, then it is likely that the leucorrhoea is a symptom of a vaginal infection.

Other symptoms are loss of appetitie, cough, difficulty in breathing, general weakness and pain in the lumbar region and calves.

Heavy, oily and viscous foods, a disordered digestion, sedentary habits and inflammation of the womb soon after childbirth, or displacement of the uterus are some of the causes of leucorrhoea.

Women past the menopause are also likely to have this disorder due to the slow degradation of the endocrine glands which secrete hormones and other products vital for body function directly into the blood.

FENUGREEK

Trigonella foenum-graecum
Methi

Ingredients

Seeds, crushed	2 tsp
Water	4 cups

Method
Mix the fenugreek seeds in the water and heat the mixture to a simmer over a low flame. Let the tea simmer for 30 minutes, then cool to room temperature and strain.
Preparation time: 30 minutes.

Dosage
1 cup, 4 times a day.

HAZARDANA

Euphorbia hypericifolia Linn.
Hazardana

Ingredients

Herb, powdered	1 tsp
Water	1 cup

Method
Stir the herb powder in 1 cup water, cover and leave overnight, then strain. *Preparation time: 8–10 hours.*

Dosage
1 cup a day.

Excessive Bleeding (Menorrhagia): This condition is characterised by excessively heavy periods. Excessive bleeding may occur because of the menopause or due to an abnormal growth, benign or malignant, in the uterus. In severe cases, it may lead to anaemia. The symptoms include regular, heavy or prolonged periods, periods that are heavier than usual, and fatigue.

Painful Menstruation (Dysmenorrhoea): Painful menstruation or dysmenorrhoea is common in girls and young women and rarely points to a disease. Its symptoms are cramp-like discomfort in the lower abdomen, back or thighs – the pain experienced may vary in intensity from mild to severe – frequent passing of urine, nausea, vomiting, diarrhoea, backache and headache.

The reasons for painful menstruation are anxiety and tension, the inflammation of the reproductive organs, namely, the womb, ovaries and the Fallopian tubes; abnormal position of the uterus; and tumour in the uterus or ovaries.

Stoppage of Menstruation: The absence or stoppage of menstruation or very slight periods is usually a consequence of pregnancy, lactation or the menopause which usually occurs between the ages of 45 and 50. Other reasons for scanty menstruation are diseases of the glands responsible for the control of ovulation, anaemia, tuberculosis, diabetes, inflammation of the kidneys, prolonged malaria and major anxiety.

ASOKA

Saraca indica
Ashoka

Ingredients

Dried bark, crushed — 15 g
Water — 1 cup

Method

Add the water to the herb and bring the mixture to a boil. Continue boiling till the liquid is concentrated to ¼ cup, then remove from the fire and cool. Strain and sweeten with sugar or honey. *Preparation time: 10 minutes.*

Dosage

1-4 tbsp a day.

Recommendation: If using fresh bark, use only ½ cup water and reduce it by boiling to 2 tbsp. This tea provides relief from excessive menstruation.

BLACK CUMIN

Nigella sativa
Kala zeera

Ingredients

Seeds, powdered — 1 tsp
Boiling water — 1 cup

Method

Put the powdered black cumin in 1 cup boiling water, cover and set aside to cool for 15 minutes. Strain and serve. *Preparation time: 15 minutes.*

Dosage

¼ cup, twice a day

Recommendation: This tea is helpful in promoting menstruation.

MARIGOLD

Calendula officinalis

Zergul

Ingredients

Flowers, granulated	1–2 tsp
Boiling water	1 cup

Method

In a covered container, steep the granulated flowers in boiling water for 15 minutes. Strain the liquid and discard the flowers. *Preparation time: 15 minutes.*

Dosage

1 cup a day.

Recommendation: Marigold tea encourages the onset of menstruation.

POMEGRANATE

Punica granatum

Anar

Ingredients

Bark, crushed	12 g
Water	1 cup

Method

To prepare pomegranate tea, cook the bark in 1 cup water till only half the water remains. Strain the decoction and take in the morning. *Preparation time: 7–8 minutes.*

Dosage

½ cup in the morning.

Recommendation: This tea controls excessive bleeding during menstruation.

EMBELIA + GINGER

Embelia ribes Burm. f. + *Zingiber officinale*
Viranga/Baberang + Adrak

Ingredients

Embelia, whole plant, powdered	6 g
Ginger, dried, powdered	6 g
Water	1¾ cups
Sugar	6 g

Method

Mix the two herbs and boil in 1¾ cups water for 15 minutes. Remove from the fire, strain and sweeten with the sugar.

Preparation time: 15 minutes.

Dosage

¾ cup a day.

Recommendation: Relieves painful menstruation.

JUNIPER + MYRRH

Juniperus communis Linn. + *Commiphora myrrha*, Nees Engl.
Abbhal/Aaraar + Mur makki

Ingredients

Juniper berries, crushed	6 g
Myrrh, crushed	6 g
Water	1½ cups

Method

Boil the herbs in the water for 15 minutes in a covered container, then strain and drink in the morning.

Preparation time: 15 minutes.

Dosage

½ cup in the morning for 10 days.

Recommendation: This tea is excellent for women suffering from painful menstruation.

INDIAN LABURNAM + JUNIPER + MADDER

Cassia fistula + *Juniperus communis* + *Rubia tinctorum*
Amaltas + Abbhal/Aaraar + Bacho/Majeeth

Ingredients

Indian laburnam rind, crushed	4 g
Juniper fruit, crushed	4 g
Madder root, powdered	4 g
Water	1 cup

Method
Add 1 cup water to the herb mixture and heat to boiling. Reduce the volume of the mixture to half by continued boiling. Filter the tea, sweeten and drink. *Preparation time: 7–8 minutes.*

Dosage
½ cup, twice a day.

Recommendation: This polyherbal tea is excellent for promoting menstruation.

More About Juniper

Egyptian physicians of the 16th century used the oil of juniper berries as a laxative. Over the centuries it has been used to treat a variety of ailments, including bronchitis, cancer, tuberculosis, gas and arthritis. But it was the 17th-century Dutch doctor, Franciscus de la Boe, who discovered the powerful diuretic properties of the berries of the juniper and in the process he also created gin.

Nausea

Nausea is a feeling of sickness without vomiting. Various causes can precipitate an attack of nausea. For example, nausea is a common occurrence in the early stages of pregnancy. Eight out of ten women suffer from it, however, only about 40 per cent experience vomiting.

Many people experience nausea while travelling by road, sea or air. This is known as motion sickness, where the movement of the vehicle prevents the signals from the eye and ear from tallying.

Headaches, including cluster headaches and migraines, may produce nausea and vomiting. Other common causes of nausea include eating or drinking too much, sudden changes of posture, most fevers, gastritis and gastroenteritis.

Somethimes disorders of the digestive tract and some chronic diseases may also produce nausea.

Several herbal teas are useful in offsetting an attack of nausea.

BLACK PEPPER

Piper nigrum

Kali mirch

Ingredients

Seeds, crushed	½ tsp
Water	1½ cups

Method

Mix the crushed seeds in the water and bring to a simmer. Remove from the heat, cover and let stand for 10 minutes before straining the decoction. *Preparation time: 10 minutes.*

Dosage

10-30 drops a day.

Note: Reduce the dose for children according to age.

PEPPERMINT

Mentha piperita Linn.
Paparaminta

Ingredients

Leaves, crushed	1–2 tsp
Boiling water	1 cup

Method
In a covered vessel, allow the peppermint leaves to steep in 1 cup of boiling water for 10 minutes. Strain the mixture and drink it hot. *Preparation time: 10 minutes.*

Dosage
1-2 cups a day.

SPEARMINT

Mentha spicata
Pahadi pudina

Ingredients

Leaves, crushed	1 tsp
Water	2 cups

Method
Heat the mixture of leaves and water to boiling, remove and stand, covered, for 10-15 minutes. Filter the extract, discarding the leaves. *Preparation time: 10–15 minutes.*

Dosage
1 cup, 3 times a day.

BALM + CHAMOMILE + PEPPERMINT

Melissa officinalis Voss + *Anthemis nobilis* Linn. + *Mentha piperita* Linn.

Rogani balsan + Babuna + Paparaminta

Ingredients

Balm leaves, ground	2/3 tsp
Chamomile blossoms, ground	2/3 tsp
Peppermint leaves, ground	2/3 tsp
Boiling water	1 cup

Method

Combine the three herbs in a container, pour the boiling water over the herb mixture, cover and let the tea brew for 10 minutes. Strain the tea and sip it slowly while it is still hot. *Preparation time: 10 minutes.*

Dosage

1-2 cups a day.

BLACK HOREHOUND + JAVA GALANGAL + MARSHMALLOW

Marrubium vulgare + *Alpinia glalanga* + *Althaea officinale*

Pahari gandana + Bara kulinjan + Khatmi

Ingredients

Black horehound plant, ground	1/3 tsp
Java galangal plant, ground	1/3 tsp
Marshmallow plant, ground	1/3 tsp
Boiling water	1 tsp

Method

Pour the boiling water over the three herbs, cover the pan and let the mixture stand for 15 minutes, then strain. *Preparation time: 15 minutes.*

Dosage

1 cup, 3 times a day.

Nervous exhaustion is an outcome of nervous tension and is caused by too much worry and stress. Stress causes the body to produce a substance called adrenalin, which prepares the body to fight the stress by releasing glucose, a source of energy, from the liver. The adrenalin constricts the capillaries, and the blood is diverted to the muscles and internal organs. Along with other changes in the body, the heart rate increases and blood pressure rises. All these changes, if prolonged, exhaust the body, leading to serious complications.

Some herbs have a soothing effect on the nervous system while restoring the natural balance of the body.

AMERICAN GINSENG

Panax quinquefolius

Ingredients

Root, shredded	½ tsp
Water	1 cup

Method

Boil the ginseng root in the water for 1 minute, then cover and set aside to cool for 15 minutes. After the standing period, strain and drink.

Preparation time: boiling time 1 minute; standing time 15 minutes.

Dosage

1-2 cups a day.

ROSEMARY

Rosmarinus officinalis
Rusmary

Ingredients

Leaves, crushed	1 tsp
Boiling water	1 cup

Method

Immerse the leaves in the boiling water, cover the vessel and let the mixture steep for 15 minutes. Remove the leaves through a strainer and drink the remaining liquid.

Preparation time: 15 minutes.

Dosage

1 cup, twice a day.

LAVENDER + ROSEMARY

Lavandula angustifolia + Rosmarinus officinalis
Dharu + Rusmary

Ingredients

Lavender blossoms, crushed	½ tsp
Rosemary leaves, crushed	½ tsp
Boiling water	1 cup

Method

To make the tea, place the herbs in a pan and pour the boiling water over them. Cover the pan and let the tea brew for 10 minutes. Strain and discard the solid matter.

Preparation time: 15 minutes.

Dosage

1 cup a day.

Neuralgia is pain that results from a nerve being compressed or irritated. In this condition, there is an intermittent attack of excruciating, shooting, stabbing or burning pain radiating along the full course of the nerve. The usual sites for this pain are the face, the back of the head, the space between the ribs, the back of the thighs (sciatica), the testes in men and the breasts in women.

Children usually don't suffer from neuralgia, but it is common among young adults. An inflammation or infection could cause neuralgia. People who have a history of gout and rheumatism and those suffering from malaria, influenza, diabetes, syphillis or mental strain are likely to have neuralgia.

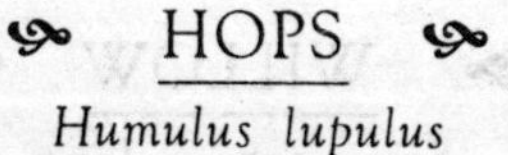

HOPS

Humulus lupulus

Ingredients

Herb	10 g
Boiling water	2 cups

Method

Steep the hops in the boiling water for 15 minutes in a covered container and strain. *Preparation time: 15 minutes.*

Dosage

1 cup, twice a day.

❧ VALERIAN ❧

Valeriana officinalis Linn.
Jalakan

Ingredients

Rhizomes/root, powdered	1 tsp
Boiling water	1 cup

Method

Prepare the infusion by steeping the herb in the water for 10 minutes with the lid of the pan closed. Then strain and discard the herb. *Preparation time: 10 minutes.*

Dosage

¼ cup, 4 times a day.

Caution: Pregnant and nursing women should not take this tea.

❧ WILLOW ❧

Salix caprea Linn.
Vivir/Malchang

Ingredients

Bark, shredded	1 tsp
Water	2 cups

Method

To prepare the decoction, boil the bark in 2 cups water in a covered vessel for 15 minutes. Then remove it from the fire and strain. *Preparation time: 15 minutes.*

Dosage

1 cup, twice a day.

In this condition, fluid that has leaked from the circulatory system accumulates in the body's tissue with attendant swelling. It is most commonly seen in the ankles and feet where it arrives by gravity, but it also occurs in other parts of the body. Prolonged standing and wearing constricting garments can produce oedema. Too much salt in the diet also contributes to this condition since salt tends to hold water and the excess fluid then travels downwards to the ankles and feet. Sometimes even a dye, say, in a sock or in a cosmetic, may induce oedema. Women may experience oedema before the onset of the menstrual period. Oedema can also result from an injury, but persistent oedema that does not disappear with rest may indicate diseases associated with the heart, kidneys and liver.

ELECAMPANE

Inula helenium Linn.

Rasan

Ingredients

Root, finely chopped	1–2 tsp
Water	2 cups

Method

Boil the finely chopped root in a covered container for 2-3 minutes, then let the mixture stand, away from the heat, for 15 minutes. Strain and drink.

Preparation time: boiling time 2–3 minutes; standing time 15minutes.

Dosage

1 cup, twice a day.

GERMANDER

Teucrium chamaedrys Linn.
Kamazariyns

Ingredients

Flowering plant, chopped	2 tsp
Boiling water	2 cups

Method

In a container with a lid combine the herb and water, close the lid and let the mixture steep for 15 minutes, then strain.
Preparation time: 15 minutes.

Dosage

1 cup, twice a day.

GOKULAKANTA

Hygrophila spinosa
Gokhulakanta

Ingredients

Root, lightly pounded	30 g
Water	2½ cups

Method

Boil the herb in 2½ cups water until the volume is reduced to 1½ cups, approximately 15-20 minutes. The lid of the vessel should be kept closed throughout the cooking time. After cooking, cool the tea, strain and drink.
Preparation time: 15–20 minutes.

Dosage

2-4 tbsp, every 2 hours.

KIDNEY BEAN

Phaseolus vulgaris Haricot
Sem

Ingredients

Dried bean pods without the seed, chopped	1 tsp
Water	1 cup

Method

Put the chopped pods into the water and boil for 2–3 minutes. Remove from the fire, cover and let stand for 15 minutes. Strain and drink the extract. *Preparation time: boiling time 2–3 minutes; standing time 15 minutes.*

Dosage.

1 cup, twice a day.

PARSLEY

Petroselinum crispum
Prajmoda

Ingredients

Whole plant, including seeds and root, ground	1 tsp
Water	1 cup

Method

Simmer the parsley in the water for 2–3 minutes, remove from the fire and cool, covered, for 15 minutes. Strain and drink. *Preparation time: boiling time 2–3 minutes; standing time 15 minutes.*

Dosage

1 cup, twice a day.

Caution: This tea is not recommended for pregnant and nursing women.

With advancing age many changes take place in the body as, for example, the termination of reproduction ability in women and diminution of sexual activity in men. Also, diseases like hypertension, diabetes, arteriosclerosis, osteoporosis (the degeneration of the bones), rheumatism, enlarged prostate and piles are more common in the elderly. The most annoying condition, however, is the development of aches and pains in various parts of the body, namely, the back and in the joints, sciatica and spondylitis. The traditional system of medicine offers some hope in terms of relieving such aches and pains. It should, however, be remembered that mental and physical activity plays an important role in postponing the onset of the problems associated with old age.

AMERICAN GINSENG

Panax quinquefolius

Ingredients

Root, shredded	½ tsp
Water	1 cup

Method

Boil the ginseng root in the water for 1 minute, then cover and set aside to cool for 15 minutes. After the standing period, strain and drink.

Preparation time: boiling time 1 minute; standing time 15 minutes.

Dosage

1 cup, 2-3 times a day.

ROSEMARY

Rosmarinus officinalis

Rusmary

Ingredients

Dried/fresh blossoms, crushed	1 tsp
Boiling water	1 cup

Method

Pour the boiling water over the blossoms, cover the vessel and steep for 5-10 minutes. Strain and drink the liquid. *Preparation time: 5-10 minutes.*

Dosage

1 cup, twice a day.

ST JOHN'S WORT

Hypericum perforatum

Basant

Ingredients

Dried/fresh blossoms, chopped	2 tsp
Water	1 cup

Method

Heat the water and the blossoms to a simmer, then remove from the fire. Cover the vessel and cool the mixture for 15 minutes before straining. *Preparation time: 15 minutes.*

Dosage

1 cup, twice a day, morning and evening for several weeks.

Peptic is the name given to any ulcer, including duodenal and gastric ulcers, which is produced by the normal digestive juices. It is an inflamed break in the mucous membrane lining of the alimentary tract. Poorly treated ulcers may result in the perforation of the stomach as in a gastric ulcer, or bleeding from the eroded blood vessel as in a duodenal ulcer. Both these conditions are dangerous.

A peptic ulcer results from too much spicy food and too much alcohol, coffee or aspirin. Nervous tension, anxiety and frustration are the other factors that can cause a peptic ulcer.

The symptoms of a peptic ulcer are a burning sensation in the upper abdomen and lower chest, weight loss due to impaired digestion and dark-coloured stool.

BAEL

Aegle marmelos Linn., Correa

Bel

Ingredients

Leaves, crushed	1 handful
Water	2 cups

Method

Soak the bael leaves overnight in the water, strain and drink the liquid. *Preparation time: 12 hours.*

Dosage

1 cup, twice a day.

FLAX

Linum usitatissimum

Alsi

Ingredients

Seeds, crushed	1 tsp
Water	1 cup

Method

Stir the crushed flax seeds in the water, cover and leave for 8 hours. Strain and drink lukewarm. *Preparation time: 8 hours.*

Dosage

1 cup before breakfast and 1 cup 30 minutes before the main meal.

GERMAN CHAMOMILE

Matricaria recutita

Babunahphal

Ingredients

Fresh/dried blossoms, crushed	1–2 tsp
Boiling water	1 cup

Method

In a covered vessel, soak the German chamomile blossoms in 1 cup boiling water for 10-15 minutes. Strain the infusion and drink as recommended. *Preparation time: 10–15 minutes.*

Dosage

1 cup, in small sips, 3 times a day between meals for several weeks.

LIQUORICE

Glycyrrhiza glabra
Mulethi

Ingredients

Sticks, shredded	1 tsp
Boiling water	¾ cup

Method
Put the shredded sticks into the boiling water and bring the mixture to a simmer. Heat for 5 minutes and remove. Strain and drink the extract. *Preparation time: 5 minutes.*

Dosage
½ cup, 3 times a day after meals for one month.

Caution: Do not continue this treatment for more than 4-6 weeks. Side effects such as swelling in the face and joints, and headaches will disappear when the treatment ends. During this treatment a salt-free diet is recommended. The elderly and those suffering from cardiovascular diseases and kidney and liver problems should not take liquorice in any form.

POMEGRANATE

Punica granatum
Anar

Ingredients

Leaves and flowers,	6 g
Water	¼ cup

Method
Grind the pomegranate leaves and flowers in ¼ cup water, strain and drink the liquid. *Preparation time: 5 minutes.*

Dosage
¼ cup in the morning.

An inflammation of the lining of a vein is known as phlebitis. This condition appears mostly in the legs. It is associated with thrombosis, a blood clot that blocks the vein, and therefore is also referred to as thrombophlebitis.

Phlebitis is caused by varicose veins, injury to a vein, prolonged inactivity, or the constriction of a vein.

Varicose veins occur when the superficial veins of the body, particularly the legs, are abnormally dilated, full of windings and elongations.

Pregnant women, obese persons and people in professions that require long periods of standing are prone to this disorder.

RUE

Ruta graveolens

Sadab

Ingredients

Herb, chopped	2 tsp
Boiling water	1 cup

Method

Steep the chopped herb in the boiling water for 15 minutes, making sure the vessel is kept covered. Strain the tea and drink as recommended. *Preparation time: 15 minutes.*

Dosage

1 cup, 3 times a day.

YELLOW SWEET CLOVER

Melilotus officinalis

Ingredients

Herb, chopped	2 tsp
Boiling water	1 cup

Method

In a container with a lid, cover the herb with the boiling water, close the lid and let the tea brew for 10 minutes before straining. *Preparation time: 10 minutes.*

Dosage

1 cup, 3-4 times a day.

More About Rosemary

Ancient Greek students wore sprigs of rosemary in their hair to enhance their memory. It was also used then, as now, as a meat preservative. Today, herbalists prescribe it for digestive and menstrual problems and for problems of old age such as arteriosclerosis. It was Isabella, Queen of Hungary, who popularised rosemary as a rejuvenating tonic. More importantly, recent studies on animals show that the oil derived from rosemary leaves can inhibit the development of some types of cancer.

The swelling of the veins in and around the anal canal is known as piles or haemorrhoids. Piles appear as small lumps which quite often bleed. The cause of external piles is usually a ruptured vein outside the anus, from straining to pass a motion. The subsequent bleeding raises a small swelling beneath the skin and clots form in the vein. Constant straining during constipation, chronic cough, obesity, pregnancy and abdominal tumours lead to internal varicose veins.

The contributory factors for haemorrhoids are hard, dry and irritant foods like chillies, irregular eating habits and riding a vehicle for a long time.

MULLEIN

Verbascum thapsus

Gidar tamaku

Ingredients

Leaves, crushed	1 tsp
Boiling water	1 cup

Method

Sprinkle the leaves in the boiling water, cover the vessel and steep for 20 minutes. Then remove the leaves by straining the mixture, and drink the extract. *Preparation time: 20 minutes.*

Dosage

1-2 cups a day, 1 tbsp at a time.

SMARTWEED

Polygonum hydropiper

Packermull

Ingredients

Dried/fresh herb, crushed	2-3 tsp
Water	1 cup

Method

Combine the herb and water and heat the mixture to a simmer. Remove the pan from the fire, cover and let it stand for 15 minutes. Strain and drink.

Preparation time: 15 minutes.

Dosage

1 cup, twice a day, morning and evening.

WITCH HAZEL

Hamamelis virginiana

Ingredients

Leaves/bark, crushed	1 tsp
Boiling water	1 cup

Method

To prepare the tea, boil the herb in 1 cup water for 2-3 minutes. Remove from the heat, cover the pan and let the mixture stand for 10 minutes. Strain and drink.

Preparation time: boiling time 2-3 minutes; standing time 10 minutes.

Dosage

1 cup, twice a day, morning and evening.

YARROW

Achillea millefolium Linn.
Gandana

Ingredients

Herb/blossoms, crushed	1-2 tsp
Water	1 cup

Method
Prepare the infusion by combining the herb with the water in a covered container. Let the mixture stand for 5-6 hours. Strain the infusion before drinking. *Preparation time: 5-6 hours.*

Dosage
1 cup, twice a day.

HOPS + VALERIAN

Humulus lupulus + Valeriana officinalis, Linn.
Jalakan

Ingredients

Hops, flowering plant, crushed	½ tsp
Valerian root, crushed,	½ tsp
Water	1 cup

Method
Place the herbs in the water, cover the pan and allow the mixture to stand for 8 hours, shaking the pan occasionally. Strain and serve. *Preparation time: 8 hours.*

Dosage
1 cup, twice a day.

Note: This tea is not recommended for pregnant and nursing women.

Prostate Gland, Enlarged

The prostate gland produces part of a man's semen and is located just below the bladder. After the age of 50, it sometimes begins to enlarge in size and compress the neck of the bladder obstructing the flow of urine. It may also develop malignant growths or tumours.

The symptoms of an enlarged prostate gland include the bladder never feeling completely empty, passing small amounts of urine, frequent passing of urine, especially at night, and the total stoppage of urine.

Cysts which exert pressure on the bladder and the infection of the bladder are some of the causes of an enlarged prostate gland.

Benign, innocent tumours of the prostate are sometimes referred to as 'prostate adenoma'. People in the age range of 55 to 70 are more susceptible to them.

STINGING NETTLE

Urtica dioica

Bichhu

Ingredients

Root, powdered	1 tsp
Water	1¼ cups

Method

Boil the powdered root in 1¼ cups water for 15 minutes, then cover the pan and set the mixture aside for another 15 minutes. *Preparation time: boiling time 15 minutes; standing time 15 minutes.*

Dosage

2-3 tsp a day.

Rheumatism is the general term for pain and swelling in the joints and muscles, aggravated by movement and pressure.

Rheumatism includes many conditions such as rheumatoid arthritis, osteoarthritis and cervical spondylosis.

Rheumatoid arthritis is a progressive destructive sm\welling of the joints. Its symptoms are stiffness and pain in the affected joints, red skin over the affected areas and limited movement.

Ostcoarthritis is a disease of late middle age, in which the protective cartilage covering the bony end undergoes wear and tear, causing excruciating pain.

Cervical spondylosis mainly affects people over the age of 40, when irreversible degenaration of the joints of the spine takes place, causing intense pain in the back of the neck or around the shoulder-blades.

ASH

Fraxinus excelsior

Kum/Sum

Ingredients

Leaves, chopped	2–3 tsp
Water	2 cups

Method

Boil the herb and water mixture for 10 minutes, remove from the heat, cover and let stand for 10 minutes. Strain the decoction berfore drinking.

Preparation time: boiling time 10 minutes; standing time 10 minutes.

Dosage

1 cup, twice a day.

BITTERSWEET

Solanum dulcamara
Anab-es-salab

Ingredients

Twigs, chopped	30 g
Water	3 cups

Method
Cook the twigs in 3 cups water till the volume is reduced to 1½ cups, then strain. *Preparation time: 20 minutes.*

Dosage
½ cup, 3 times a day.

COUCH GRASS

Elymus repens Linn
Doorva

Ingredients

Rhizomes, chopped	1–2 tsp
Water	4 cups

Method
Combine the rhizomes with the water and bring to a boil. Cover and continue boiling the mixture for 10 minutes, then set it aside for 30 minutes, away from the heat. Then strain and drink. *Preparation time: boiling time 10 minutes; standing time 30 minutes..*

Dosage
1 cup, 4 times a day.

DANDELION

Taraxacum officinale Weber

Ingredients

Leaves, shredded	1–2 tsp
Water	1 cup

Method

Boil the herb and water mixture for 1 minute, then remove the source of heat, cover the pan and let the tea brew for 15 minutes, and strain.

Preparation time: boiling time 1 minute; standing time 15 minutes.

Dosage

1 cup, morning and evening for 4-8 weeks, during the spring and winter months.

PARSLEY

Petroselinum crispum

Prajmoda

Ingredients

Plant with stem, chopped	1 handful
Water	3 cups

Method

Add the parsley to the water and bring to a boil. Reduce the heat, cover the pan and simmer for 30 minutes. Strain the decoction and drink twice a day. *Preparation time: 30 minutes.*

Dosage

1 cup, twice a day.

Caution: Parsley tea is not recommended for pregnant and nursing women.

STINGING NETTLE

Urtica dioica
Bichhu

Ingredients

Dried leaves, crushed	1–2 tsp
Water	1 cup

Method
Combine the leaves with the water and bring the mixture to a boil. Boil for 2 minutes, then remove from the fire, cover and set aside to cool for 15 minutes. Strain the decoction, and the tea is ready.
Preparation time: boiling time 2 minutes; standing time 15 minutes.

Dosage
1 cup, twice a day for 4-6 weeks, 2-3 times a year.

WILLOW

Salix caprea
Vivir/Malchang

Ingredients

Dried bark, crushed	2–3 tsp
Water	4 cups

Method
Boil the bark for 5 minutes, then cover and let stand away from the heat for 15 minutes. When the tea has cooled, strain and drink.
Preparation time: boiling time 2 minutes; standing time 15 minutes.

Dosage
1 cup, twice a day.
Helpful hint: Use only the bark of a tree that is 2-5 years old.

Boils (Abscess): A boil is an abscess within the skin. It is a raised, pus-filled pocket caused by a bacterial infection. The bacteria enter the skin either through a break in the surface resulting from a cut, scratch or puncture, or through a hair follicle, a sac-like structure, or through a sweat gland. The bacteria multiply rapidly and kill the follicle and the surrounding cells in the skin, which form pus. As the pus increases, the boil grows till it comes to a head, when it bursts, ejecting the pus. Boils commonly occur on the breasts, buttocks, face and neck, but are most painful when located on the ear, upper lip, finger or nose. Sometimes they may be accompanied by fever.

Eczema (Dermatitis): This is an inflammation of the skin which begins with redness of the skin due to the dilation of its blood vessels. Fluid collects in the skin causing it to swell, itch and blister. Where the skin is thin, as on the face, neck, the backs of the knees or the insides of the elbows, the blisters burst quickly. But where the skin is thick, as on the palms and soles, they burst much later.

All types of allergic itching skin rashes come under the category of eczema. Contact dermatitis develops on the exposed skin of people sensitive to a particular irritant such as the synthetic dyes used in cosmetics, detergents and furniture polish. Foods, like nuts, berries, tomato products, milk and eggs may cause a flare-up of eczema.

Measles: A highly contagious disease, measles occurs mainly in children. It is caused by a virus that spreads either by direct contact or by the germ-laden air breathed out by patients. The first indication of the infection is the onset of high fever, cough, reddening of the eyes and a runny nose, followed by a rash of dark-pink raised spots. The rash first appears behind the ears or on the neck and spreads in blotches over the entire body by the fourth day. In the final phase of the disease the skin of the spots begins to peel, after which the body temperature drops to normal.

Prickly Heat: In hot and humid weather, rashes sometimes appear on the skin causing a pricking sensation with severe itching. This condition is called prickly heat or heat rash.

Excessive sweating causes the skin cells to swell and block the sweat ducts. The trapped sweat is what causes the rash. Small red eruptions or blisters appear on the abdomen, chest and back, in the skin creases and in the areas where clothing is tight. Wearing loose cotton clothing, lying under a fan and frequent cool water baths without soap help to relieve the symptoms. Overweight people and those whose diet consists of rich and spicy foods are more susceptible to prickly heat.

Scabies: This skin disease is caused by the female mite parasite which burrows into the skin to lay its eggs. This results in intense and constant itching. The favourite sites for the parasitic attack are where the skin is soft and thin, as between the fingers and toes, the insides of the knees, elbows and wrists, the buttocks, breasts and genitalia. Itchy pimples appear wherever the mite lays its eggs. When scratched, these pimples turn into sores. Untreated, the condition becomes chronic. Scabies is transmitted readily by skin-to-skin contact with an infected person.

Urticaria (Nettlerash): Blood vessles in the skin release fluid which collects in the skin and its underlying tissues, causing them to swell. The resulting eruptions resemble a mosquito bite or the sting of a nettle, thus giving urticaria its common name, nettlerash. These swellings are manifested as reddish or pale patches, and are associated with itching and pain.

Allergy to certain foods like shellfish, eggs, nuts, fruits and drinks may give rise to an attack of urticaria. Allergies may also arise from insect bites or stings, or from antibiotics such as penicillin or streptomycin.

ENGLISH WALNUT

Juglans regia
Akhrot

Ingredients

Walnut meat and dried leaves, crushed	2 tsp
Water	1 cup

Method
Soak the walnut meat and leaves in the water for 5-10 minutes. Strain and drink as recommended.
Preparation time: 5–10 minutes.

Dosage
1 cup, twice a day for several weeks.

Recommendation: English walnut tea is recommended for the treatment of eczema or dermatitis.

NEEM

Azadirachta indica, A. Juss
Neem

Ingredients

Leaves, crushed	2 tbsp
Water	2 cups

Method
Add the neem leaves to the water and bring to a boil in a covered container. Boil for 15 minutes, then strain. Add sugar or honey if desired. *Preparation time: 15 minutes.*

Dosage
¼-½ cup, 4 times a day.

Recommendation: Excellent for skin diseases in general and boils in particular.

PURPLE TEPROSIA

Tephrosia purpurea
Sarphankha

Ingredients

Tender leaves, crushed	1 tbsp
Water	1 cup

Method

Boil the leaves in the water for 10 minutes, keeping the container covered. Strain the decoction and discard the leaves. *Preparation time: 10 minutes.*

Dosage

½ cup in the morning.

Recommendation: Purple teprosia tea can be taken to cure dry eczema.

SAFFLOWER

Carthamus tinctorius
Kusum

Ingredients

Flowers, chopped	1 tbsp
Boiling water	2 cups

Method

Cover the flowers with the boiling water, close the lid of the pan and let the mixture stand for 15 minutes. Remove the flowers and drink the strained liquid.
Preparation time: 15 minutes.

Dosage

1 cup, twice a day.

Recommendation: Advised for children suffering from skin diseases in general and measles in particular.

BLACK CUMIN + JUNIPER

Nigella sativa + *Juniperus communis* Linn.
Kala zeera + Abbhal/Aaraar

Ingredients

Black cumin seeds, crushed	½ tsp
Juniper berries, crushed	½ tsp
Water	¾ cup

Method
Combine the ingredients and boil till the liquid is reduced to ⅓ cup. Strain and drink in the morning.
Preparation time: 4–5 minutes.

Dosage
⅓ cup, in the morning.
Recommendation: This tea is an effective cure for urticaria.

CORIANDER + CUMIN + POMEGRANATE + ROSE

Coriandrum sativum Linn. + *Cuminum cyminum* Linn. + *Punica granatum* + *Rosa damascena*
Dhania + Safed zeera + Anar + Gulab

Ingredients

Coriander seeds, pulverised	11 g
Cumin seeds, pulverised	11 g
Pomegranate root, pulverised	11 g
Rose root, pulverised	11 g
Water	1 cup

Method
Soak the herbs overnight in the water. Strain and drink in the morning after sweetening it with a little sugar.
Preparation time: 8–10 hours.

Dosage
1 cup in the morning.

CHIRATA + COMMON FUMITORY + EAST INDIAN GLOBE THISTLE + JUJUBE + PURPLE TEPROSIA

Swestia chirata + *Fumaria indicus* Linn. + *Echinops indicus* Linn. + *Ziziphus jujuba*+ *Tephrosia purpurea*
Chirayata + Pitpara + Gorakmundi + Unnab/Ber + Sarphankha

Ingredients

Chirata, whole plant, ground	4 g
East Indian globe thistle, whole plant, crushed	4 g
Jujube fruit, crushed	6 numbers
Purple theprosia, whole plant, crushed	4 g
Sugar	6 g
Water	2 cups

Method
Put the first four ingredients in a pan and then add the water. Cover the pan and raise the mixture to a boil. Continue boiling for 20 minutes. Strain the tea, discarding the solid matter. Sweeten the liquid extract with the sugar and drink twice a day.
Preparation time: 20 minutes.

Dosage
¾ cup, twice a day.

Recommendation: This tea relieves the symptoms of scabies, itching and acne.

Stomach or abdominal pain is usually a symptom of a minor disorder like indigestion, but may also arise from a possible serious illness such as gastroenteritis, tonsillitis, urinary disorders, appendicitis or ulcers.

Pain arising from digestive disoders usually occurs in the upper or lower abdomen and is a result of diarrhoea, overeating, vomiting or nausea.

Herbal teas and extracts work very well in relieving stomach pain caused by indigestion. For pains that point to a more serious illness, it would be best to consult a medical practioner.

CORIANDER

Coriandrum sativum Linn.
Dhania

Ingredients

Seeds, crushed	15 g
Water	½ cup

Method

Heat the mixture of seeds and water in a covered container till the liquid is reduced to 3 tablespoons. Strain the tea and cool.

Preparation time: 5–7 minutes.

Dosage

1-3 tsp, twice a day.

Recommendation: This decoction relieves acidity in the stomach.

FENNEL

Foeniculum vulgare
Saunf

Ingredients

Seeds, crushed	1 tsp
Boiling water	1 cup

Method
Let the fennel seeds stand in the boiling water for 10-15 minutes in a covered container. Strain the tea and drink hot.
Preparation time: 10–15 minutes.

Doage
1 cup, 2-3 times a day.

PEPPERMINT

Mentha piperita
Paparaminta

Ingredients

Leaves, crushed	15 g
Boiling water	2 cups

Method
Pour the boiling water over the leaves, cover and let the tea brew for 5-20 minutes. For light tea steep for 5 minutes; 20 minutes for stronger tea. Strain the tea and drink hot or warm.
Preparation time: 5–20 minutes.

Dosage
1-2 cups a day.

Recommendation: This tea is excellent for treating stomach spasms and gastric distress.

SPEARMINT

Mentha spicata
Pahadi pudina

Ingredients

Leaves, crushed	1 tsp
Water	2 cups

Method
Combine the spearmint leaves and the water and raise the mixture to a boil in a covered container. Remove from the heat and let the tea stand for 15 minutes. Strain the decoction before drinking. *Preparation time: 15 minutes.*

Dosage
1-2 cups a day.

Recommendation: Spearmint tea, like peppermint tea, is useful in relieving gastric distress and stomach spasms.

CARDAMOM + FENNEL + MINT

Elettaria cardamomum + *Pimpinella anisum* Linn. + *Mentha arvensis*
Choti elaichi + Saunf + Pudina

Ingredients

Cardamom, powdered	1 g
Fennel seeds, powdered	1 g
Mint leaves, ground	1 g
Water	2 cups

Method
Boil the herb mixture in 2 cups water in a covered pan for 15 minutes. Remove from the heat and allow it to stand for 15 minutes before straining.
Preparation time:boiling time 15 minutes; standing time 15 minutes.

Dosage
½ cup, twice a day.

CORIANDER + GINGER

Coriandrum sativum + *Zingiber officinale* Rosc.
Dhania + Adrak

Ingredients

Coriander powder	½ tsp
Ginger powder	½ tsp
Boiling water	1 cup

Method
Combine equal parts of the powdered herbs to make 1 teaspoon of herb mixture. Pour boiling water over it, cover and allow the tea to infuse for 5-10 minutes. Strain, and the tea is ready.
Preparation time: 5-10 minutes.

Dosage
1 cup, twice a day.

Recommendation: This tea is excellent for relieving indigestion in children.

More About Garlic

Many ancient civilisations used garlic as a food and for its medicinal properties. It was believed that its strong odour was protection against infectious illnesses as well as vampires. Raw mashed garlic was put on the soles of the feet to cure bronchitis, and garlic cooked in milk was considered a good remedy for intestinal worms. During the construction of the ancient pyramids of Egypt, the workers were fed tonnes of garlic to keep up their strength.

The best way to overcome mental or nervous tension is to avoid stress and follow a healthy lifestyle – a sensible diet, regular exercise and enough sleep. It is advisable to try to solve problems as they arise rather than worrying about them over a prolonged period.

Some of the symptoms of mental tension are fatigue and exhaustion, irritability, insomnia, hypertension and ulcers. If not controlled, mental tension can often lead to various heart diseases.

The herbal teas and extracts given here have a calming effect on the nerves.

BALM

Melissa officinalis

Rogani balsan

Ingredients

Dried leaves, crushed	2-3 tsp
Boiling water	1 cup

Method

In a vessel with a cover, combine the crushed leaves and boiling water, close the lid and allow the mixture to cool for 10 minutes. Then strain and drink morning and evening.

Preparation time: 10 minutes.

Dosage

1 cup, twice a day.

BITTER ORANGE

Citrus aurantium
Khatta

Ingredients

Blossoms, leaves or peel, shredded	1–2 tsp
Boiling water	1 cup

Method

Put the herb into the boiling water, cover and set aside for 10-15 minutes. When the tea has cooled, strain and discard the herb reserving the liquid. *Preparation time: 10–15 minutes.*

Dosage

1 cup, twice a day, morning and evening.

CHAMOMILE

Anthemis nobilis
Babunah

Ingredients

Flowers, crushed	15 g
Boiling water	2 cups

Method

For light tea, steep the flowers in boiling water for 5 minutes. For stronger tea, soak the flowers in a covered vessel for 20 minutes. When the tea is ready, strain and drink.
Preparation time: 5–20 minutes.

Dosage

1-2 cups a day.

Caution: Chamomile tea is not recommended for children under two years of age.

Urine, Blood in the (Haematuria)

The presence of blood in the urine could be due to inflammation of the filters in the kidneys, (called Nephritis in medical terminology), or inflammation of the bladder (called Cystitis) or the presence of stones in the kidneys.

Nephritis is caused by auto immune disease. In this condition, the blood escapes through leaks in the damaged filter beds, resulting in smoky-coloured or red urine. The volume of urine is small and the patient may develop a puffy face, severe headache and backache. Blood in the urine due to the presence of stones in the kidneys occurs when the stones get dislodged and travel downwards, scratching the urinary passage which bleeds and thus imparts a brown colour to the urine. If the scratching occurs in the urethra, the urine will acquire a bright red colour and there may be pain and difficulty in passing urine.

BARLEY

Hordeum vulgare

Jau

Ingredients

Seeds, crushed	25 g
Water	4 cups

Method

Mix the crushed barley seeds in the water, cover the pan and boil for 20 minutes. Strain and take as recommended.

Preparation time: 20 minutes.

Dosage

1 cup, 3 times a day.

Urine, Blood in the (Haematuria)

VASAKA

Adhatoda vasica Ness

Adusa

Ingredients

Leaves	12 g
Water	1 cup

Method

Grind the vasaka leaves in the water and strain the liquid before drinking it. *Preparation time: 5 minutes.*

Dosage

1 cup, twice a day.

More About Senna

In the ninth century, the caliph of Baghdad commanded his physician, Mesue, the Elder, to produce a laxative that worked better than the ones already available. The physician gave the caliph senna, which worked very well indeed, for senna is a powerful laxative and should be taken only in the amounts prescribed.

Pain and a burning sensation which urinating point to hyperacidity of the urine, or a disorder of the kidneys. In the latter case, law back pain is frequent

FLAX

Linum usitatissimum

Alsi

Ingredients

Seeds, crushed	15 g
Water	2 cups

Method

Soak the seeds in the water for 5-20 minutes in a covered pan. Strain and drink hot or warm.

Preparation time: 5 minutes for light tea; 20 minutes for strong tea.

Dosage

1-2 cups a day.

GOLDENROD

Solidago virgaurea

Ingredients

Whole plant, ground	1–2 tsp
Water	4 cups

Method

Boil the herb in a covered pan for 2 minutes. Remove from the fire and cool for 10-15 minutes. Strain and drink. *Preparation time: boiling time 2 minutes; standing time 10–15 minutes.*

Dosage

1 cup, 2-4 times a day.

Urination, Painful (Dysuria)

ONION

Allium cepa

Piyaz

Ingredients

Bulbs, crushed	6 g
Water	2 cups

Method

Combine the bulbs with the water and bring the mixture to a boil. Continue boiling till the quantity of water is reduced to 1 cup. Cool the decoction and strain.

Preparation time: 15 minutes .

Dosage

1 cup, twice a day.

PURSLANE

Claytonia portulaca Linn.

Kulfa/Khursa

Ingredients

Leaves, crushed	1 tsp
Boiling water	½ cup

Method

Make an infusion by steeping the purslane leaves in the water in a covered pan for 12 hours. Strain the infusion, discard the leaves and drink 1½ teaspoons of the remaining extract twice a day. *Preparation time: 12 hours.*

Dosage

1½ tsp, twice a day.

SENNA

Cassia angustifolia
Senna

Ingredients

Leaves, finely chopped/ powdered	10–30 g
Water	4 cups

Method
Pour the water over the herb and allow the mixture to stand for 5-6 hours. Strain and serve. *Preparation time: 5–6 hours.*

Dosage
1 cup, 4 times a day.

CUCUMBER + CUCUMBER

Cucumis utilissimus Roxb. & Linn. + *Cucumis sativus* Linn.
Kakri + Khira

Ingredients

Cucumber seeds	6 g
Cucumber seeds	6 g
Water	½ cup

Method
Powder the cucumber seeds in a mortar, then boil the powder in the water for 2 minutes. Strain the mixture and drink in the morning. *Preparation time: 2 minutes.*

Dosage
½ cup a day.

Urine Retention (Anuria)

As a result of acute inflammation of the kidneys there is a likelihood of the complete obstruction of the flow of urine giving rise to a condition known as anuria or urine retention.

The symptoms associated with this disorder are dryness of the mouth, twitching of muscles, insomnia and restlessness.

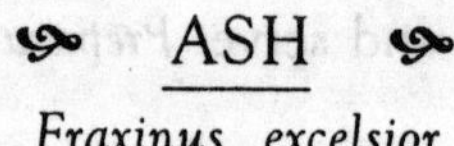

ASH

Fraxinus excelsior
Kum/Sum

Ingredients

Dried leaves, chopped	2–3 tsp
Water	2 cups

Method
Boil the ash leaves in 2 cups water in a covered vessel for 15 minutes, then remove from the heat and set aside to cool for 1 hour. Strain.
Preparation time: boiling time 15 minutes; cooling time 1 hour.

Dosage
1 cup, twice a day.

BEARBERRY

Arctostaphylos uva–ursi

Ingredients

Leaves, powdered	4 tsp
Water	4 cups

Method

Mix the powdered leaves in the water, cover and leave for 12 hours. Do not heat or boil the mixture but drink cold after straining. *Preparation time: 12 hours.*

Dosage

1 cup, 2-3 times a day.

NUT GRASS

Cyperus rotundus

Nagarmotha

Ingredients

Tubers, powdered	6 g
Water	2 cups

Method

Soak the powdered tubers for 12 hours in the water in a covered vessel, then strain. *Preparation time: 12 hours.*

Dosage

1 cup, twice a day.

SPREADING HOGWEED

Boerhaavia diffusa

Punarnava

Ingredients

Whole plant, crushed	1 tsp
Water	1 cup

Method

Combine the herb and water and bring the mixture to a boil. Cover and simmer for 10 minutes then remove from the fire and cool for another 10 minutes before straining.

Preparation time: boiling time 10 minutes; standing time 10 minutes.

Dosage

1–2 tsp a day.

STINGING NETTLE

Urtica dioica

Bichhu

Ingredients

Leaves, crushed	3–4 tsp
Boiling water	4 cups

Method

Let the nettle leaves steep in the boiling water for 15 minutes in a covered pan, then strain the liquid extract.

Preparation time: 15 minutes.

Dosage

¼ cup, 4 times a day.

Vomiting is a common symptom with many causes, some of which are emotional upsets, indigestion from excessive eating and drinking, pregnancy, intestinal worms and constipation.

Excessive vomiting can lead to dehydration or the loss of water in the body.

CHAMOMILE + EUROPEAN CENTAURY + FENNEL + LEMON BALM + PEPPERMINT

Anthemis nobiliis, Linn. + *Centaurium umbellantum* + *Foeniculum vulgare,* + *Melissa officinalis* + *Mentha piperita*
Babunah + Bans Keora + Saunf + Aspurk + Paparaminta

Ingredients

Chamomile flowers, ground	½ tsp
European centaury plant, ground	½ tsp
Fennel seeds, crushed .	½ tsp
Lemon balm plant, ground	½ tsp
Peppermint plant, ground	½ tsp
Hot water	1 cup

Method
Combine the herbs and pour the water over them. Cover and stand for 15 minutes and strain. *Preparation time: 15 minutes.*

Dosage
1 cup, twice a day.

Caution: Not recommended for children under the age of two.

Vomiting

❧ CHAMOMILE + EUROPEAN ❧ CENTAURY + PEPPERMINT + SPEARMINT + WORMWOOD

Anthemis noblis, Linn. + *Centaurium umbellantum* + *Mentha piperita* + *Mentha spicata* + *Artemisia absinthium*

Babunah + Bans keora + Paparaminta + Pahari pudina + Vilayati afsanthin

Ingredients

Chamomile floweres, ground	½ tsp
European centaury plant, ground	½ tsp
Peppermint plant, ground	½ tsp
Spearmint plant, ground	½ tsp
Wormwood plant, ground	1 tsp
Boiling water	1 cup

Method

Combine all the herbs and add 1 cup boiling water. Cover the pan and leave for 15 minutes. Strain the infusion and discard the herbs. *Preparation time: 15 minutes.*

Dosage

1 cup, 3 times a day.

❧ *More About Holy Basil*

Native to India, Holy Basil has been in cultivation since ancient times. The Egyptians used it to treat snakebites and to relieve the aches and pains of arthritis. The Greeks used it as a health drink and as a sedative.

BLACK HOREHOUND + CHAMOMILE + MEADOWSWEET

Ballota nigra + *Anthemis nobilis,* Linn + *Filipendula ulmaria*
Pahari Gandana + Babunah + Vanpushp

Ingredients

Black horehound plant, ground	1/3 tsp
Chamomile flowers, ground	1/3 tsp
Meadowsweet plant, ground	1/3 tsp
Boiling water	1 cup

Method

Combine the herbs in 1 cup boiling water and let the mixture steep for 15 minutes. Strain the mixture, and the tea is ready to drink. *Preparation time: 15 minutes.*

Dosage

1 cup, twice a day.

Recommendation: This tea controls vomiting during pregnancy.

More About Horehound

Medieval Europeans used horehound to protect themselves from evil and the spells of witches. For thousands of years herbalists have used it as an effective remedy for coughs. In 19th-century America, it was also prescribed for colds, bronchial problems, intestinal worms and menstrual complaints. Horehound has other uses too. The English flavour their ales with it, while for the Jews, it constitutes a bitter herb at the Jewish Passover.

A wound is a result of the penetration of the skin with a sharp edge, puncture by a nail, pin or a sharp object, a cut or a bruise from a fall or a road accident. If the blood gushes from the wound, it indicates an injury to an artery. If there is a feeling of numbness or a tingling sensation, then it points to an injury to a nerve.

LEMON

Citrus limon

Bara nimboo

Ingredients

Lemon fruit, halved	1 number
Water	2 cups

Method

Cover the halved fruit with 2 cups water and bring to a boil. Continue boiling for 15 minutes, then remove from the fire and allow the tea to stand for a further 10 minutes. Strain and drink as recommended. *Preparation time: boiling time 15 minutes; standing time 10 minutes.*

Dosage

1 cup a day.

Helpful hint: Vitamin C and bioflavonoids present in the yellow outer skin and the white inner skin of the lemon stregthen the capillaries, thus accelerating the healing process.

TURMERIC + ALUM

Curcuma longa

Haldi + Phitkari

Ingredients

Turmeric, powdered	3 g
Alum, powdered	½ g
Cow's milk	½ cup

Method

Combine the turmeric and alum with the milk and heat the mixture to about 70°C and drink as recommended.

Preparation time: 5 minutes.

Dosage

½ cup a day for several days.

STINGING NETTLE

Urtica dioica

Bichhu

Ingredients

Dried leaves, crushed	2 tsp
Water	1 cup

Method

Boil the mixture of nettle leaves and water for 5 minutes. Remove from the heat, cover the pan and allow the mixture to stand for 1 hour. Strain and drink.

Preparation time: boiling time 5 minutes; standing time 1 hour.

Dosage

⅓ cup, 3 times a day.

Helpful hint: The paste of the leaves of the Holy Basil (tulsi) acts as a coagulant when applied to a bleeding wound. Infected wounds respond well when strips of papaya are applied locally.

A sedative is a preparation that subdues excitement or pain, and makes the patient calm, quiet and composed without inducing sleep, though drowsiness may result in some cases.

Sedatives reduce anxiety and restlessness in people who suffer from diseases like chronic asthma, stomach ulcers and high blood pressure.

There are several herbal teas that lessen the severity of pain and have a calming affect.

HAWTHORN + LIME + MISTLETOE

Crataegus oxycantha + *Citrus bergamia* Ris er Poi + *Viscum album*

Ban sangli + Nimboo + Banda

Ingredients

Hawthorn fruit/flowers, ground	¼ tsp
Lime flowers, ground	1¼ tsp
Mistletoe plant, ground	½ tsp
Boiling water	2 cups

Method

Mix the herbs and pour the boiling water over them. Let the mixture stand for 15 minutes, then strain.

Preparation time: 15 minutes.

Dosage

1 cup, twice a day.

HYSSOP + LAVENDER + LEMON BALM

Hyssopus officinalis Linn. + *Lavandula angustifolia* + *Melissa officinalis*

Zufa yabis + Dharu + Aspurk

Ingredients

Hyssop plant, crushed	⅔ tsp
Lavender flowers, crushed	⅔ tsp
Lemon balm plant, crushed	⅔ tsp
Water	2 cups

Method

Combine the herbs and add the mixture to the water. Boil for 1 minute, remove from the heat, cover and let it stand for 15 minutes. Strain the decoction before drinking.

Preparation time: boiling time 1 minute; standing time 15 minutes.

Dosage

1 cup, 4 times a day.

More About Hyssop

This plant of the mint family has been in use as a medicine for centuries. It is mentioned in the Bible, and both Hippocrates and Galen recommended it for treating bronchitis. Many herbalists also prescribe it for coughs and colds, sore throats and fevers.

Herbal preparations which have the power of restoring the normal tone and vigour of the body, particularly after an illness, are known as tonics. Different tonics tone up different organs of the body. For example, there are tonics for the stomach, heart, kidneys, liver, intestines, nerves and blood vessels.

Chamomile tea acts as a stimulant while liquorice tea has rejuvenating properties when used for a long period. It is effective in quenching thirst and is useful in relieving stomach disorders.

Ginger tea is a stimulating carminative and excellent for relieving digestive disorders and respiratory problems, including coughs and colds. It is warming for the whole system.

The regular use of Indian gooseberry tones up the whole body and promotes health and vigour.

Health drinks act in much the same way as tonics in that they help to keep the body healthy, providing it with energy and vigour.

BELERIC MYROBALAN

Terminalia belerica

Bahera

Ingredients

Fruit pulp, crushed	3 g
Water	1¼ cups

Method

Bring the herb and water mixture to a boil, cover and cook for 15 minutes, then strain. *Preparation time: 15 minutes.*

Dosage

1-2 tsp a day.

CHAMOMILE

Anthemis nobilis
Babunah

Ingredients

Flowers, crushed	1 handful
Boiling water	2 cups

Method
Steep the flowers in boiling water for 15 minutes in a covered vessel, then strain and drink hot or warm.
Preparation time : 15 minutes.

Dosage
1 cup, twice a day.

Caution: Chamomile tea is not recommended for children under two years of age.

GREATER CARDAMOM

Amomum sabulatum Roxb.
Bari elaichi

Ingredients

Whole cardamom, powdered	2 g
Boiling water	2 cups,
Assam tea leaves	½ tsp

Method
Prepare the tea by steeping the Assam tea leaves in the boiling water in a covered vessel for 10 minutes. Strain and add the powdered cardamom before drinking.
Preparation time : 15 minutes.

Dosage
1 cup a day.

Recommendation: An excellent tonic for the heart and liver.

WINTER CHERRY

Withania somnifera
Ashva ganda/Akri

Ingredients

Fruit, powdered	1–4 g
Water	1 cup
Milk	1 cup

Method
Combine the milk and water and add the powdered herb. Boil this mixture in a covered container for 15 minutes, then strain and add a little honey or sugar to the liquid extract.
Preparation time: 15 minutes.

Dosage
1-2 cups a day.

GINGER + INDIAN GOOSEBERRY

Zingiber officinale Rosc + *Emblica officinalis* Gaertn.
Adrak + Amla

Ingredients

Ginger rhizomes, powdered	½ tsp
Indian gooseberry fruit, powdered	½ tsp
Water	8 cups

Method
Add the powdered herbs to the water and boil the mixture till the volume is reduced to 4 cups. Cool the tea, then strain and add a little honey to it before drinking.
Preparation time: 40 minutes.

Dosage
1 cup, 4 times a day.

Bibliography

Bakhru, H.K., *Foods That Heal*, (1993), *Herbs That Heal*, (1992) Orient Paperbacks, Delhi.

Central Council for Research in Unani Medicine, *Handbook of Common Remedies in Unani System of Medicine*, New Delhi (1976).

Chopra, R., Nayar, S. and Chopra, I., *Glossary of Indian Medicinal Plants*, Council of Scientific & Industrial Research, New Delhi (1956).

Chopra, R.N., Chopra, I.C. and Varma, B.S., *Supplement to Glossary of Indian Medicinal Plants*, Publications & Information Directorate, CSIR, New Delhi (1969).

Conway, D., *The Magic of Herbs*, Granada Publishing, St. Albans, (1977).

Dastur, J., *Everybody's Guide to Ayurvedic Medicine, Medicinal Plants of India & Pakistan*, D.B. Taraporeval Sons & Co., Bombay, (1972).

Devaraj, T.L., *Speaking of Ayurvedic Remedies for Common Diseases*, Sterling Publishers Pvt. Ltd., New Delhi, (1985).

Fluck, H., *Medicinal Plants & Their Uses*, W. Foulsham & Co., London, (1976).

Hameed Saheb, Hakim H.A., *The Complete Book of Home Remedies*, Orient Paperbacks, Delhi, (1982).

Institute of Chinese Materia Medica, *Medicinal Plants of China*, Chinese Academy of Traditional Chinese Medicine, WHO Manila, (1989).

Jain, S.K., *Medicinal Plants, National Book Trust*, New Delhi, 1968.

Lakshmipathi, A. Ed., *Hundred Useful Drugs*, Arogya Ashram Samithi, Madras, (1973).

Miller, S., *A Natural Mood Booster*, Newsweek, (1987).

Nadkarni, K.M., Nadkarni, A.K., *Indian Materia Medica*, Popular Prakashan, Bombay, (1976).

Satyavati, G.V., Raina, M.K., and Sharma, M. Eds, *Medicinal Plant of India, Vol. I.*, Indian Council of Medicinal Research, (1976).

Satyavati, G.V., Gupta, A.K., Tandon, N. and Seth, S.D. Eds, *Medicinal Plants of Inida, Vol. II*, Indian Council of Medicinal Research, (1987).

Sweet, M., *Common Edible & Useful Plants of the West*, Naturegraph Co., Healdsburg, California, (1962).

Taylor, V.E., *Drugs of Choice: The Therapeutic Uses of Phytomedicinals*, Pharmaceutical Products Press, New York, (1994).

Thomson, A. Ed., *Healing Plants: A Modern Herbal*, McGraw Hill Co., UK, (1978).

Verma, G.S., *Miracles of Indian Herbs*, Rasayan Pharmacy, Delhi, (1960).

Weiner, M., *Weiner's Herbal*, Quantum Books, California, (1990).

Index

In this index the herbs are listed by their common English name, followed by the Indian name in italics, wherever available.

Index